LIVING
is HARD

But Life Is Easy

LIVING *is* HARD

But Life Is Easy

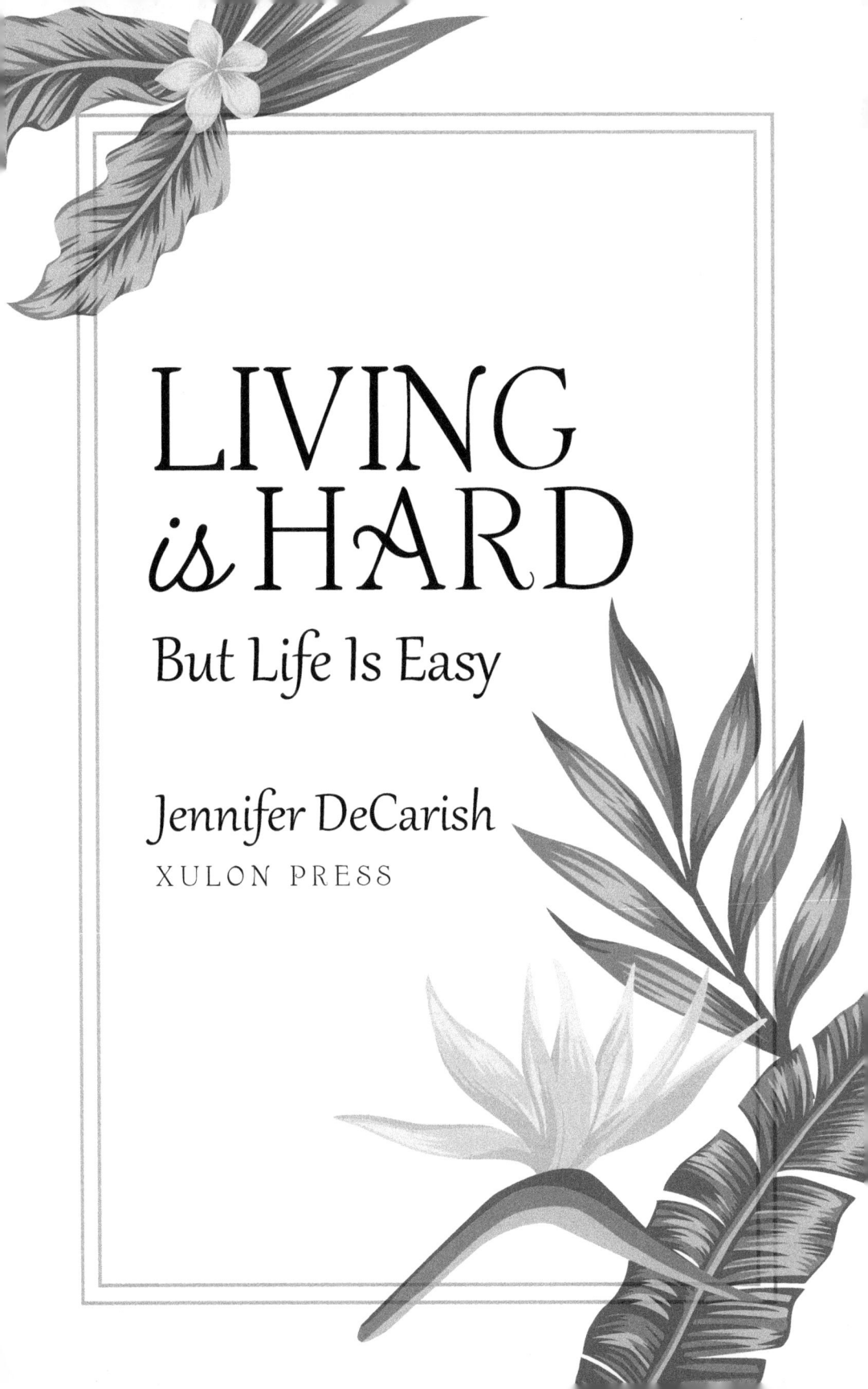

Jennifer DeCarish

XULON PRESS

Xulon Press
2301 Lucien Way #415
Maitland, FL 32751
407.339.4217
www.xulonpress.com

© 2020 by Jennifer DeCarish

All rights reserved solely by the author. The author guarantees all contents are original and do not infringe upon the legal rights of any other person or work. No part of this book may be reproduced in any form without the permission of the author. The views expressed in this book are not necessarily those of the publisher.

Unless otherwise indicated, Scripture quotations taken from the Good News Translation (GNT). Copyright © 1992 American Bible Society. Used by permission. All rights reserved.

Library of Congress Control Number:

Paperback ISBN-13: 978-1-6312-9611-6

Ebook ISBN-13: 978-1-6312-9612-3

Acknowledgement

I hereby acknowledge my family, especially my two children, Germaine and Orinthea who encouraged and supported me to make this book possible. To my friends who kept reminding me to finish the book and prayed for me, I say thank you. I also acknowledge Pastor Dan King who taught and inspired me in the things of God and encouraged me to continue to magnify the name of the Lord and Dr. DaCosta who encouraged me to write what the Lord has instructed me. I express my gratitude to my students who also challenged me and encouraged me to write this book.

Background

About six years ago, I had a conversation with the Lord. I believe it was in 2013-2014 when I went through some very tough times. I was in debt, lost properties, lost homes, and lost my marriage. I began to beat myself and blame myself for all that had happened. During this time, I drew closer to the Lord and asked Him how to carry on in life. It was then I heard the phrase, "Living is hard, but life is easy". I pondered this phrase, and I remember saying to the Lord: "What is the meaning of all of this because nothing in my life now is making any sense?" Then, I began to ask the Lord where the easy part was of what I was going through. In a couple of months, it dawned on me that the Lord had given me the title of a book.

I started putting ideas on paper, praying for answers but ran out of ideas. I could not understand what was going on. So, I put away all the rough draft for about a year. I started again in 2015 to work on the manuscript to work on the manuscript. I did not put much effort because I was working two jobs at the time. I went back to school while I was going through a divorce. After the divorce, I started working on the book again. This time, I had to change a few things because the Holy Spirit had shed a new light regarding the content of the book.

The Holy Spirit had me thinking about life as a gift and how unappreciative we are at times. The Lord started to deal with me and told me that we only treasure gifts we can see. The things we see are temporary and what we cannot see is eternal. I started to understand what He was saying and began to realize how casually we take our life instead of treasuring the gift of life. We do whatever we want, go wherever we want and live however we want. I began to search the scriptures to see what the Word say about life.

I learned a few things, and the most important is that Life belongs to the creator of the universe and not to man. That is, life belongs to God. He gave life freely; He had a plan for each of us before we were created. Even after Adam sinned, the Lord had a redemption plan for man. So then, God gave us life, and he had a plan in place as to how we should live the life He gave us. In addition, He gave us free will and consequences for whatever choices we make. I realized then that I had made plenty choices and have reaped some of the consequences.

The Lord started to drop phrases and sub-headings in my spirit. I would write these down, search the scriptures and listen to what the Lord had to say. Then, I documented what the scriptures say and additional revelation of the scriptures. The more I searched, the more I found. I realized that I got into a lot of trouble because of lack of knowledge and disobedience. I realized how wrong I was doing things my way. It was no wonder I got into so much trouble. If I knew then what I know now, I would have saved myself a lot of headache and sleepless nights. Life was given to be cherished and lived the way that the Lord planned it.

Table of Contents

Acknowledgement v
Background vii
Introduction xi

Chapter 1
The Gift Of Life 1
   Living For God 2
   God's Purposes And Plans For Our Lives 9

Chapter 2
The Effect Of Spiritual Growth On Life 13
   The Effect Of Worrying On Living 15
   Fear And Its Effect On Living 18
   Peace And Harmony Benefits 20

Chapter 3
Changes And Transition In Life 27
   Seasons And Opportunities In Life 29
   Sowing With Purpose 35

Chapter 4
Faith And Its Influence On Living 37
   Trust In God 40
   Complaining And Its Effect On Living 42
   Gratitude And Appreciation 42

Chapter 5
Procrastination And Time Management 45
   Harvest And Timing 49
   Past Experiences And Mistakes: Effect On Living 51

Chapter 6
Wisdom And Hearing God 55
    The Effects Of Obedience On Living 60

Chapter 7
Knowing Our Purpose And Identity 65
    Dreams, Visions And Talents 67

Chapter 8
Humility And Respect 71
    The Effect Of Favor On Living 74
    How Faithfulness And Consistency Affect Our Lives 75

Chapter 9
Anger 79
    How Conflicts Affect Living 81
    Rebellion 82
    How To Deal With Trials And Temptations 83

Chapter 10
Courage 85
    How To Identify The Enemy: Strategy To Win 86
    Prayer As A Weapon Of Choice 88
    Repentance To Gain Recognition In The Kingdom 91
    Forgiveness To Access Mercy 92

Chapter 11
Relationship And Shaping Lives 95
    Relationship With Christ And Living 97
    Idolatory And Its Effect On Living 100

Chapter 12
How Wealth Affects Living 103
    Authority 104
    How Choices Affect Living 106
    How Covenants And Pledges Affect Living 107

Conclusion 109

Introduction

Very often, we hear people say life is rough and complicated. After asking why, their response is that it is difficult to get ahead, and others may say life is too unpredictable. Further discussion may require differentiating life from living. Emotion is often used to create, describe and define life. For example, some may say "life is lovely" or with a hint of sarcasm "I am breathing." This is no more than an attempt to explain or describe of a difficult life or a great life. This phrase often provokes our thoughts and imagination to figure out what life is and how it was originated.

Such curiosity leads to asking of why, how, where and when questions with the hope of getting a satisfying answer. Many people will give their opinion of these questions by referring to their life experiences, encounters, knowledge, assumptions, perception and relationships. Some people rely solely on personal experience and their understanding to explain the meaning of life. Questions such as: Who am I? Where did I come from? Why am I here? What is my purpose here? are questions that many people are trying to get answered. This compulsive instinct and enthusiasm create pressure on the mind, and people become curious to get answers to their questions.

As many people continue to weigh in on life, its challenges and uncertainties, some may conclude that life itself is complex. Interacting with their challenges and making difficult choices create the need to know what life is about. An awareness of the environment for many people makes much sense to those who question the meaning of life. Living may be defined as "fully alive, not dead, functional, growing, reproduce and adapt to an environment" (Webster's Dictionary). The limitations of the human intellect create a tendency to define life by describing life and how individuals are affected personally.

Many people have tried to define living in concrete terms by referring to material things and their interaction with these things. Others have focused on the essential things that human needs to survive and function. Since the beginning of time, theorists, scientists and philosophers have encountered great challenges as they try to define life and living. The human mind is limited. As we try to figure out how we got here, it gets extremely complicated and thought provoking.

The physical characteristic of life is used then to explain living and non-living. Even at this point, we all have questions because we need more information. Therefore, questions about our origin and the origin of life can only be answered by God the creator. Genesis tells us that God is the creator of life. Acts 17:28 states, "In Him we live, move and have our being." God is worthy to receive glory, honor and power because He created all things. These things were given life and existence by God (Revelation 4:11). It is the Lord who gives breath and creates life (Psalm 104:30).

Life is a force that operates within us, and the source of this force is God. He is the orchestrator and the giver of life. Psalm 36:9 says, "God is the giver of life." This means that life is a gift. We know that God gives only the best. So then, we should treasure the unmerited gift of life. Since life is a gift, we ought to respect our life and the lives of others. We all know that life has a source, and the source is God according to the Book of Genesis..

Life can only be explained and understood when people are connected to God and have a relationship with Him. That is when He starts revealing mysteries to us to help us to understand. A purpose-driven life is led by God (John 15:1-6), life is purposeful when we abide in God ("who abide in me and I in him bears much fruit"). That means

Introduction

reproduction is a vital function of life. The best definition of life is given by the Lord. In Him, we move and have our being: that is life.

Life according to God's plan is the expression of the intelligence that flows from God to man. Man depends on this spiritual flow to move and operate in the Earth's realm. Living becomes hard when a person develops the attitude of independence and disrupts the flow of life from the Lord to us. Also, when we focus on the physical things around us and put our trust in men, we are disconnecting ourselves from the source of life. God's word tells us to trust in the Lord with all our hearts and lean not unto our own understanding.

Life and its meaning get rather complicated when we look for explanation within ourselves and from other people. This lends itself to confusion and frustration. Proverbs 3:5 and John 15:3 remind that we can do nothing without God. Life was predestined by our father in heaven. We were not created to live independently of Him; not trusting Him creates hardship and limitations in our lives. Living is hard when the Kingdom of God cannot come to us because of these hinderances we have created.

Life is wonderful when God is expressed in our daily living. Matthew 6:10 states "Thy kingdom come; thy will be done on earth as it is in heaven." God's plan for our lives is accomplished when we allow Him to work in and through us. The word says, "If we are willing and obedient, we shall eat the good of the land." This is one of the many promises God has made for us (Isaiah 1:19).

Chapter 1
The Gift Of Life

Life is a gift that God the father handed down to mankind. In the beginning he said, "Let us make man in our own image" (Genesis 1:26). Therefore, God has created life to be a precious and great gift. Consequently, that life is God and God is life. We cannot separate them. There is no life without God, and life cannot exist without God. On close examination of the word life, the second and third letters, which spells "if," suggest or express this uncertainty.

Therefore, it would then be reasonable to say life is God's will, and mankind received this undeserved gift. Life was given freely because God is love. Jesus said, "I have come to give abundant life" (John 10:10). Life is made of several fundamental principles and is a deliberate act of God. Life is a gift because it was designed by God before the foundation of the world. It was not our choice to be born. It was by the perfect will and design of the Lord.

It is our responsibility to discover God's design for our lives to achieve a success and make good choices. Our choices in relationships, achievement and lifestyle will determine the outcome of our lives. Living becomes difficult when we set our own goals and standards for our lives and disregard God's purposeful will for us. Our destiny was planned and designed before the foundation of the world, according to Jeremiah 1:5 and Ephesians 1:4. Therefore, God knows what is best for us according to His intended purpose for our lives.

Hypothetical

God gave us life not to destroy it but, to preserve it by doing His will. Life is more than just for living.

Living For God

According to Romans 8:13," The just shall live by faith." Hebrews 11:6 tells us that we cannot please God without faith. He is a rewarder of those who comes to Him believing that He is God. We all know the story of Abraham our forefather and how he believed God and lived by faith. In every single encounter, we see him obeying and honoring God. In every situation, God came through for him supernaturally and impressively. He always depended on God for everything, and we are also given the same opportunity.

We can experience the Lord in our own situations. If we put our trust in God, the Lord comes through for us in unimaginable ways. We can depend on Him to solve problems, reverse catastrophe, break curses, heal and deliver us from the plots of the enemy. The greatest spiritual secret in life is to trust in the Lord (Proverbs 3:5-6). Life is easy when we trust in the Lord. Living will become a burden and uncertain when we depend on others to guide and solve problems. Independent and selfish living only leads to destruction.

As human beings, we need to acknowledge that we are vulnerable and weak. We need the wisdom of the Lord in our everyday living. If we fail to acknowledge who we are in Christ, we will continue to live defeated and stressful lives. Life is hard when people experience pain and difficulty. Some people lack the wisdom to seek the Lord. Trying to live independent of the Lord will only bring more trouble into our lives. We are setting ourselves up for failure when we do things our way.

The spirit of independence will allow us to do things according to our own understanding, thoughts, perceptions and motives. Seeking to please people will not please God. God tells us in His word (Zechariah 4:6,) "not by might nor by power but by my spirit said the Lord." God expects us to do things, make decisions and live our lives according to His will. We must cooperate with God to get the things He promised us. Life is easy when we live God's way.

Living is hard when we do things our way, take measures to solve our own problems and most importantly leave the Lord out of the plan. We readily follow the instructions and manuals for the operation of machinery and objects, but we ignore the manual for our lives. The purchase of equipment requires the use and understanding of the manufacturer's instruction. The equipment could be damaged or operate poorly and sometimes will not operate at all if the manufacturer's instructions are not followed.

In addition, the clothes we wear comes with care instructions—for example, hand wash in cold water or dry clean only. We follow these instructions to preserve our clothes, but how about preserving our lives? Some people place more emphasis on the preservation of things more than their own self. It is unfortunate that we spend more time and energy on trivial things and neglect seeking the manual that teaches us to how to care for ourselves: the word of God. This is the same thing with our life: It is a gift that comes with instructions; we accept the gift but ignore the manual.

The word of God delivers the instructions for our life. If these instructions are not followed, living becomes hard and at times meaningless. We need wisdom, knowledge and understanding to enjoy the gift that is life. We must follow God's manual for our lives to live life to its fullest. The word of God is our instruction manual; it teaches us about the intricacies of life. Life presents highs and lows, but we should learn how to overcome them. Every detail in the manual needs to be adapted into our lives for easy living. We must go to God to obtain guidance and direction to prevent errors in our walk.

Living becomes easy when we speak to God, listen actively and record what He says about our lives. Living is easy when we make wise choices daily that can only come through the words of God, praying and seeking Him. Wisdom is the word of God appropriately applied to our lives daily so we can live as God intended. Accuracy and success in our daily lives require God's wisdom. We need the wisdom and direction from the Lord to prevent us from walking in error. It makes more sense, then, for us to allow His plan to be accomplished through us. So, not allowing our wondering heart to depart from the will of God is a wise decision on our part.

He loves us with an everlasting love, but we sometimes suffer needlessly by making wrong decisions in life. We cannot keep our lives; the Lord is the keeper of our lives. So then, if He is the keeper of our lives, He knows exactly what we need. Let us be purposeful in our lives to seek the Lord in every areas of our lives. We should let the Lord know every day that we love and need Him. By so doing, we are showing Him that He is our everything and nothing matters but Him. We ought to seek the Lord all the days of our life and make Him our treasure and reward.

We cannot love the Lord if we do not know Him. We can know the Lord by spending time with Him. Spending time with the Lord allows to hear Him and follow His directions and plans for us. He knows us fully; even with our flaws and faults, He loves us unconditionally. It should be our prayers to ask the Lord to help us to love Him and seek after Him rather than seeking after man. The love of man is limited, conditional and not genuine. Unfortunately, many people seek the love and approval of man and are disappointed when this love fails.

God's love never fails or gives up on us. We should live and seek God's approval for our lives. Life will become easy for us as we do so. A deeper revelation of His love for us increases our enthusiasm to know more about Him. The more we know of Him, the more we want to know and seek Him. Knowing and loving the Lord will give us a passion to please Him because we realize we are only safe in Him. The word says, "If you abide in me and my words abide in you, you shall ask what you wish and it will happen" (John 15:7).

Living is easy when are drawn to the Lord always. He wants us to hold onto Him in every situation because He never let go of us. The word tells us that we are in the palm of the hand of God. The goal then should always be to remain in close connection to the almighty. Everything we need is in Him; miracles are happening all the time.

Living for Christ is the better life, that is everlasting life with Him. He is the only firm foundation; living is easy when He is the foundation of our lives. He has given us foundational principles in His word. These principles are the 10 commandments: the guiding principles of life (1 John 1:5, Exodus 20, Deuteronomy 5). A violation of these core foundational principles results in disciplinary actions. Broken systems are likely to result in the release of curses into the life of the violator.

Curses threaten the very essence of life by creating/causing diseases, life stressors, depression, financial hardship, damaged relationships and ultimately may lead to destruction of life––physical, emotional or spiritual. The product of such turmoil and uncertainty will make life difficult. It serves us well to remember that God's word is life. By feeding our spirit daily with the Word of God, we learn how to live and preserve our life in Him.

The lack of God's word is the recipe for self-destruction. That is, we are neglecting the most important nutrient to sustain life. This may lead to spiritual weakness and fatigue. Individuals who allow Jesus to take charge of their lives will find living easy. Those who live independently or contrary to the lead of God will encounter a difficult life. According to Psalms (37:23-24), "The steps of a good man are ordered by the Lord." The Lord keeps his feet firm. "Those individuals whose feet are not ordered by the Lord are at risk of stepping into error and destruction. There is no vision except that of the Lord" (Proverbs 29:18).

Living is difficult when we live to gratify the flesh and strive to fulfill selfish ambitions. According to James 5:16-22, the desire of the spirit is contrary to the desire of the flesh. The spirit and the flesh are in constant conflict; therefore, we can always avoid this conflict by living by the spirit. Living by the spirit means our behavior is not controlled by the law but the Holy Spirit.

Life is easy living by the spirit because the fruits of the spirit will rule our lives. The fruit of the sprit are joy, love, peace, patience, kindness, goodness, faithfulness and self-control. It is easier to seek and find the Lord when we live in the spirit because we are living in Him. Therefore, in Him we live, move and have our being. We should not overlook the fact that our life is in God.

Living in Him also means we commune with Him and follow His leading when we remain in His presence. Living is easy in His presence because no evil can come near His dwelling. In His presence, there is fullness of joy and at His right hand are pleasures forevermore (Psalm 16:11). Jesus is the peace and joy giver. Out of the presence of God is confusion, turmoil and difficulty. Living is difficult without the presence of God and the peace of God. Outside the presence of the Lord is sadness, pain, weakness and bondage. On the other hand, in the presence of the Lord there is strength, power, and freedom.

The spirit of God will take over our lives when we allow the Lord to rule our lives. He overwhelms us with his presence, and then, we experience real love and peace. There the Lord makes all things work together for the good of those who remain in His presence and put their trust in Him. Even when the storms of life rages, we are secure in His arms because He will never leave us or forsake us (Hebrews 13:5). Many are looking for this peace and joy, but they are looking in the wrong places. Some have turned to drugs and illicit lifestyles to obtain happiness. The pleasure they receive is from material and temporary things. The joy of the Lord is everlasting.

His overwhelming presence reaches to the greatest heaven and below the earth. Those who live in the spirit experience this great love and happiness. Those who operate in self or flesh are faced with frustration, discouragement and difficulty with life. They experience constant battles, storms and other unrest; they are unable to experience the joy of the Lord because they are not connected to the Spirit of Christ. The desire for flesh and worldly things keeps them in bondage. Those who are in the flesh are unable to enjoy rest in the Lord.

The Word tells us the spiritual life offers rest for the weary and tells us how to deal with the yoke. Jesus said, "my yoke is easy and my burden is light" (Matthew 11: 28-30). Living by the spirit encourages us to give the burden to Jesus Christ. Living is difficult when we carry the burden. Those who live in the flesh experiences hardship (According to Psalm 91:1, living is difficult when we are not in the place God has called us to be. The Lord wants us to dwell with Him and rests in Him.

He has assured us that when we rest in Him, He becomes our refuge and our fortress. In the presence of the Lord, we are saved from the snare of the fowler and from the deadly pestilence. Isaiah 61:3 tells us that God promises to make us new. He promises to give us "beauty for ashes and joy for despair." Many of us try to disguise and pretend, but we can only pretend so long. Even though some wear masks and live in pretense, they will become unhappy because the love of God is not able to shine. Living in the flesh will not attract the glory of the Lord because He is a spirit and those who worship must do so in the spirit.

Situations and circumstances in our lives can sometimes affect our thought process and affect our decisions. Therefore, we need to live holy lives so that the Lord can use us for His glory. Failure to recognize the presence of God can cause discouragement and disappointment, making life difficult. Our heavenly father controls the affairs of men. The Bible tells us the in the presence of the Lord there is fullness of joy, and at His right hand, there are pleasures forevermore.

There is power and deliverance in the presence of God. His presence brings happiness, joy, gladness and peace. In His presence, we are protected from dangers and harm. Psalm 91:1 tells us that whosoever dwells in the presence of God will find rest in the shadow of the almighty.

The presence of God provides us with the full acknowledgement of His mercy, grace and faithfulness. God will reveal deep secret things to those who are in his presence. Daniel reveals that only God in heaven reveal mysteries (Daniel 2:28). God's presence offers us safety, security and freedom. There is power and deliverance in the presence of God. In His presence, we are protected from dangers and harm. Psalm 91:1 tells us that whosoever dwells in the presence of God will find rest in the shadow of the almighty.

We are called to be holy vessels so that the Lord can shine through us. According to 2 Timothy 2:21, those who cleanse themselves from things that are dishonorable will become like instruments of special purposes. That is, they will be made holy and useful for the Lord's work. The Lord can only use us if we are holy. Paul wrote to the church at Ephesus and encouraged them to separate themselves from what is evil and do good. Those who allow themselves to be vessel of dishonor cannot please God.

Living is hard for those who live unclean lives because the spirit of the Lord cannot dwell with them. Those who are considered vessels of honor are ready to advance the kingdom of God. Those whom God approves are devoted to His work. These are the people who finds living easy because they are living for the Lord. Paul encourages us to live in peace with all men and be holy because without holiness no man can see God (Hebrew 12:14).

Living is hard when we speak incorrectly and lie intently. Any variation from the truth is detrimental to our lives. Flattery is false speech that is destructive to both the giver and the receiver. God hates lies and the distortion of the truth (Proverbs 21:23; Proverbs 6: 16). Those who uses divisive words are engaging in dividing people. Division usually brings strife; this can impact our lives positively and negatively. Spoken words that brings division are usually gossip, slander and destructive criticisms. Godly words are nourishment to our souls, words of wrath take life slowly from our souls by reducing nourishment.

Evil words destroy friend and family. Words of love and wisdom strengthens relationships. The tongue is like a fire; it can create a world of wickedness and destroy the rest of the body (James 3:6). The believer should speak kind, sobering and helpful words because this will improve the health of the believer. Indulging in evil and unkind words will destroy the believer. On the day of judgment, everyone will give an account of their spoken words. According to Matthew 12:27, words can either condemn or acquit us. The words of the Lord are not empty, they are life. Obeying the words of the Lord will bring us long life.

God's Purposes And Plans For Our Lives

We are not here by chance; we were created by God and for a particular purpose in a specific time. He has a perfect plan in time for every one of us. He expects us to live and give everything to Him no matter what we encounter in life. It should be our priority to inquire of the Lord as to our purpose here on earth. Every person needs to discover their identity and purpose in life.

Knowing your purpose allows you to walk in your destiny. Not knowing your purpose may lead to frustration, disappointment and anxiety. God determines our purpose in life, we should bear this in mind. The Lord will bring to pass whatever our purpose is in life when we allow His orchestration. He sometimes reveals our purpose through divine encounter, direction and through His word. At other times, He may use inward prompting; on other occasions, he uses visions and divine revelation. God's plan for us present and future is one of hope and prosperity (Jeremiah 29:11).

Sometimes we assign ourselves tasks or place ourselves in situations that drains and saps our energy. We fail because we neglect seeking the Lord and following His directions. In 1 Samuel 30: 8, David asked the Lord if he should pursue the raiders, the Lord told him to pursue. He pursued, overtook and recovered all. Sometimes people meet resistance to accomplish an activity or task because God was not consulted, and He did not approve. Often, we only seek the counsel of God when we fail, but by seeking God first, we would have averted the shame and the loss especially when dealing with finances.

Wisdom teaches us to consult with the Lord before making decisions as some may result in irreparable damages. Exercising wisdom will remind us to ask of the Lord before deciding on a matter. In any event, the Lord will help us to make the right decisions that lead to success.

In many instances, especially when our minds are bombarded with thoughts and ideas, we are at risk for jeopardizing a good outcome. Only the Lord can help us to make the right decisions, and the sooner we realize, the better the outcome. We may need to fast and pray depending the nature of the situation: some situations can only be resolved with prayer and fasting (Matthew 17:21).

In any circumstance, we always need the Lord's intervention. We need the Lord all the time because we cannot rely on ourselves to make any decision. Jesus said He is the way the truth and the life (John 14:6). This is another example that life is a gift from God, an undeserving gift. It is unproductive to live life without purpose. Living without purpose is living a life of emptiness and waste. We cannot do anything without Lord, we cannot walk, talk or think without Jesus. We cannot survive a minute without Him. The breath we breathe belongs to Him, and we cannot exist without Him.

We are not our own; therefore, we are not capable of making decisions independent of Him. Living without Jesus is like a branch disconnected from its vine, it will wither and die. Only He can walk with us, calm our fears and carry us to a place of safety. It is difficult to understand why we often do things without Him being a part of decisions. He wants to talk to us and wants us in return to share our hearts with Him.

Jesus enjoys sharing our lives; living is easy when He takes permanent residence in our lives. He can only do so when we allow Him. Jesus has all the answers we need: why do we ask people when only He knows all things. Many people call a friend first when they are faced with challenges. Our friends do not have the answer; we must go to the Lord first.

God has predestined our purpose in life; therefore, we are encouraged in His words to wait on Him for direction and answer to our every concern. He is the giver of life dreams and aspirations. He has

The Gift Of Life

the vision and blueprint for our lives; therefore, living without Him is living without direction, purpose and sustenance. Many people chose to live that way, but it does not take long for them to realize that trouble is approaching and make the change. We cannot do things on our own because we not created to live without God. He must guide us continually and lead us through this life because only He knows the journey.

God desires to have us in the palm of His hand if we allow Him. He will take us where He desires according to His plan and purposes. He is working continuously in our lives and waiting for us to allow Him to do what He does best. The Lord wants us to allow Him to bring out the best in us.

Chapter 2

THE EFFECT OF SPIRITUAL GROWTH ON LIFE

Spiritual growth is a divine promise given to the children of God. It enables us to grow in the wisdom and knowledge of God. God's desire is for us to grow physically and spiritually. This promise and power from God help us to experience the divine will of God and avoid the evil of this world. The avoidance of evil will help us to develop faith, goodness, knowledge and self-control according Peter. Self-control will help us to develop perseverance, brotherly kindness and love. As a baby grows in the natural, we are expected to grow in the spiritual (1 Peter 2:2).

The baby grows, matures and become an adult who assumes full responsibility. 1 Corinthians 13:11 states, "When I was a child, I spoke as a child; I understood as a child, I thought as a child; but when I became a man, I put away childish things." God expects us to grow in the knowledge and grace of Jesus, according to 1 Peter 2:2. It is our responsibility to grow in many dimensions. Jesus grew in wisdom, statue and favor with God and all people (Luke 2:52).

We are expected to increase our knowledge and understanding in the word of God. As we increase in the knowledge of the word, we should decrease in the frequency and severity of sin. Spiritual growth enables us to increase in practicing the character of Christ.

This will increase our faith and trust in God. In 1 Corinthians 11:1, Jesus expects us to follow Him as the example by which we should live. Living with the Holy Spirit within us means the life of Christ is within us. We are made anew and the capacity to grow is in us.

Living is hard when there is no spiritual growth because the old is not gone to make way for the new. Living by the Spirit of God allows the flesh to be subjected to God, and the sinful nature will not be gratified. Spiritual growth occurs as we read the word of God daily. The word of God is alive and active. The word can teach us, rebuke, correct and train us in the way we should go. Living becomes difficult when we refused to be trained by the Lord and becomes rebellious.

A rebellious person will do things that are contrary to the spirit. Spiritual growth allows a conflict between the sinful nature and the Spirit. Being led by the spirit, we will be led to do the things of the spirit and not the flesh. The Holy Spirit will guide and control us, and we will live according to the word. This will enable us to bear the fruits of the spirit.

The concept of bearing fruits is expressed in several places in the Bible. In Matthew 13:23, Jesus tells the story of a sower who went out and sowed seeds. Some of the seeds fell on rocky and hard ground; others fell on grounds that were receptive, but weeds choke the seed before it could take root. The soil represents the condition of the heart of people who hears the gospel. It is, therefore, safe to say that living is hard when our hearts are hard and we become rebellious and do things our own way.

A broken and a contrite heart He will not despise (Psa. 51:17). To bear fruits, we need to become more like Jesus. Spending time in the word will eventually change our lives. Spending time with Jesus will allow us to know Him better, and His thoughts will be our thoughts. We are required to read the word, digest the word and incorporate the word in our lives. Then, we will become fruitful and others will see the Lord in our lives.

According to Galatians 5: 22-23, the fruit of the spirit is love, joy, peace, longsuffering, kindness, goodness, faithfulness, gentleness and self-control. Living is easy when we fellowship with Christ. As we fellowship with Christ, others will see the fruits of the spirit within us. The condition of the heart is our responsibility. Proverbs 22:6 and Ephesians 5:1 tells us to be imitators of God. God wants us to maximize our living to the fullest. As we continue to dream bigger and think higher, we can achieve prosperity. A Godly relationship is made up of three parts: God, you and a person. God is working in you and through you, therefore, your everyday focus should be on God because our focus is narrow, and we can only work on a few things at a time. To live a healthy and a happy life, we must focus daily on Godly things. That is, God is in everything we do.

We are called to imitate Christ; we must pattern our lives after Him. We need to live each day in Christ. Our life and living are complicated as well; therefore, we need direction to function. Some people may experience slow spiritual growth, while others may grow speedily. We ought not to compare ourselves with others but look to Christ our redeemer. We should all strive to be doers of the word. We need mentorship as we grow; we should pray and ask the Lord to help us to find helpers.

In the New Testament, Paul mentored Timothy. Mentors are people we invite into our lives to correct, instruct, encourage, train, coach and help us to grow, and be the person has called us to be. Living is difficult without direction; therefore, we all need mentors who live godly and reputable lives. Their lives should be above reproach (1 Timothy 3:2). Our lives should be a mirror image of the word of God as we learn to grow spiritually.

The Effect Of Worrying On Living

Worry may be defined as giving way to anxiety by allowing your mind to dwell on your troubles. In Matthew 6: 26-27, we are encouraged not be anxious about our life, what we shall eat or drink, or about what your body what we shall wear. Living is easy when we obey the Word of God and cast all your cares on Jesus. Psalm 55:22 tells us that if we cast our cares on the Lord, He will sustain us. He will never let the righteous be forsaken. Peter encourages (Peter 5:7) us to cast all our cares on Him because He cares for us.

To live a worry-free life, we need to look beyond our situation and focus on Jesus. Great and mighty is our God, He is a burden bearer and a heavy load shifter. According to Proverbs 12:25, "worry will rob your happiness and kind words will cheer you up." There is nothing too hard for Him to do. Only Jesus can change our situations. He is our shelter in the times of storm. The storms of life will always come unexpectedly to us, but not to the Lord.

Storms are designed to destroy and interrupt our lives, but it is the Lord who has the final say. We must realize that there is a purpose for every storm and be mindful that God always prepare us for the storm. Although we may not be able to stop the storm, we can determine their duration. If we take our focus off the storm and place our focus on the creator, the storm may either cease or pass quickly. The scripture tells us that whatever the enemy meant for evil, the Lord will turn around for the good of those who trust Him.

Many storms will come to test us, and others will come to strengthen us. It is in our best interest to stand still and see the salvation of the Lord (Exodus 13:1). Whenever a storm comes into our life, it is time for us to shift our focus from the storm to Jesus the one who calm the storm. We should never lose focus on our destiny because some storms are destiny destroyers. On the opposite side of the storm lies our destiny, our health, our prosperity, our deliverance and our victory.

Therefore, we cannot afford to lose focus, the very storm is designed to throw us off course. Storms sometimes serve as a director as well as a distracter, and it is only when our focus is on Jesus that the purpose of the storm is manifested. Some storms are meant to propel us into our destiny, and others are designed to block us. Knowing God's purpose for our life will help us to determine the intent of a storm. Many times, the enemy will send a storm to destroy us, but God will change the direction and the impact of the storm in our favor (Romans 8:28).

There was a storm on the water while Jesus was in the boat. The disciples became afraid, and Jesus rebuked the storm (Mark 4:39). We cannot afford to lose our focus during the storm because Jesus speaks to storms.

Once we take the focus off ourselves and focus on Jesus, He will direct us and bring us to safety. God also allow storms in our lives to realign us, to take us from a place of complacency to a place of action and mobility. The plan of the Lord includes moving us from stagnation to growth and production.

Even if we find ourselves at Lo-debar (a lonely and desolate place) the Lord will visit us and provide for us. Sometimes we find ourselves in a place indecision, a crossroads where we desperately need the hand of God to work. Storms may be physical or spiritual. Whatever form or direction they decide to take, we should not be concerned because Jesus is in control. Situations will arise when our backs are against the wall and life seems overbearing. That is, we often need the Lord to move mountains and part the red seas in our lives. God will sometimes allow a storm in our lives for us to go to the other side. Many times, our breakthrough lies on the other side, and without the storm, we would never move into our destiny.

There is a purpose for every storm; God would never let us go through anything in life before first preparing and protecting us. We must remember always that a storm can arrive at any time, and multiple times: storms are not in our control. God promises to take care of us, and His miracles are based on His promises (Deuteronomy 31:6-8). Fear will prevent us from reaching our destiny; living becomes easy when we trust in God. We should replace fear with faith in our daily lives.

Abraham lived by faith and was more convinced about the word of God than Sarah's womb situation. In our daily lives, God is always present in our storms, He was in the fiery furnace with the three Hebrew boys. He will never leave us or forsake us (Deuteronomy 3:8). Our natural ability, strength, power, wisdom and intellect will not control the storm; we need God's supernatural intervention. Therefore, we must trust God. Proverbs 3:5 says: "Trust in the Lord with your whole heart and lean not on your own understanding."

Jesus is the creator of the universe and controls everything. He sometimes reveals what our problems are and directs us to our blessing on the other side. Storms sometimes serve as indicator that a miracle is awaiting.

It is important to look for the blessing during the storm. Living is easy when we trust God to bring us through the storm safely. Some storms serve to promote or elevate us from a lower to a higher spiritual dimension and draw us closer to Jesus. The same happened for John the revelator. He was in a storm of loneliness and depression, but God elevated him. God always have the solution before a problem, and the answer before the question.

Testimony

Personally, I have learned to hold on to Jesus in the storms of life. I have come to realized that I cannot change anything by worrying. In addition, the more I would worry the worse the situation became. So then, instead of worrying I asked the Lord to see me through a divorce, the passing of love ones and even when those who claimed they love abused and rejected me. There are many days I thought I would not make it, but today I am still here because of the goodness of God. I can testify that in my lonely days, days of not having enough food the Lord made provisions. I can stand up and tell the devil: this cannot break me; God will deliver me. He is my provider.

Fear And Its Effect On Living

Fear is the enemy of faith. It may be defined as dread or terror, but the scriptures counsels us against fear. To know God as the Holy One is healthy fear. To fear God is considered an awesome respect, obedience and service. Healthy fear of God enables to access and enjoy the blessings of the Lord. To be successful in life, we need wisdom. The fear of the Lord is the beginning of wisdom (Proverbs 9:10). Fear in this sense is like the knowledge of God. Fear helps us to do the will of God.

People without knowledge of God cannot please Him. Living is hard for those who do not know God and has a relationship with Him. The fear of God to these individuals is that of wrath and judgment, but to those who know Him, it is reverence and worship. Living is hard when people anticipate dread, terror and displeasure. God commands us in the scriptures not to fear or worry. The phrase "fear not" occurs many times in the scriptures. The Lord knows that the enemy uses fear to intimidate, distract and scare us. If we become fearful and weak, our victories will be limited. Hope and enthusiasm concerning the things of God will be reduced.

Living is hard when our hope is decreased. Decreased hope can lead to hopelessness and depression. Therefore, the Lord has reminded us several times to be hopeful and trust Him. He said to those who are fearful, be strong, fear not because He the Lord will come with vengeance and recompence to save you. The blind shall see and the deaf shall hear. The lame shall walk and streams of water shall flow in the desert (Isaiah 35: 4-6).

The Lord does not want us to think about tomorrow because tomorrow will take care of itself (Matthew 6:34). Living is easy when we seek the Lord because He will deliver us from all our fears. The Lord promised that in the middle of our thoughts and our inabilities, His love and comfort will enlighten us and directs us. This will alleviate all our fears. We should not fear what men can do to us because the Lord is on our side (Psalm 118:6). The Lord wants us to declare daily that He is our helper and not men. Living is easy when we depend on the Lord and not worry.

Testimony

I was paralyzed with the fear of flying for many years. I thought I was the only person, but I met a nurse who said whenever she is flying, she becomes short of breath and begins to panic with fear. She too narrated how claustrophobia has destroyed her life because she cannot live a normal life. Someone told me that the enemy knows your calling in life and one of his strategies is to use fear to block or stop you. So, I was determined that this was never going to happen to me and decided to use faith in God to fight fear. If I must minister to people about the goodness of God, then I must depend on God's protection. The ministry that God has called me to entails travelling. Therefore, whenever

I am afraid, I put my trust in God. Now I am flying wherever I need to go, resting assured that God is with me.

Peace And Harmony Benefits

According to Matt. 5:9, blessed are the peacemaker for they will be called the children of God. He admonishes us to live peaceably with all men. Jesus is the peace giver—where there is peace, we can find harmony. The life of the believer should be harmonious so the spirit of God can bear witness. Living becomes difficult when we lack self-control. We need to be sympathetic and kind to each other. This is a characteristic of Christ that others will see in us.

Believers dealing with the unsaved should remember that they were unsaved at some point in their lives. Striving to win arguments can sometimes cause quarrels. Believers need to stay away from strife, quarrel and anger. We should approach people with meekness, especially unbelievers. A meek person will continue to do things even though they produce hardship. Living becomes easy when believers work to produce unity, peace and harmony. A meek person avoids envy (James 3:13-18).

Envy will ruin peace. Living is difficult when there is a lack of peace and harmony. Jesus is the Prince of Peace. John 14:27 "My peace I leave with you, my peace I give to you, I do not give you as the world gives, do not be troubled and do not be afraid." Peter reminded us to cast all our anxieties on Him. Life is easy when we live a life free of fear and anxiety. The Lord told us how to experience peace by controlling our thoughts. We are to think about whatever is true, whatever is honorable, whatever is right, whatever is pure, whatever is lovely, whatever is good and worthy of praise.

So, if we practice these things, we will have peace because the God of peace will dwell in us (Philippians 4: 6-9). The peace of God gives strength; it gives you the will to guard your heart. In the presence of God, there is peace. We will have peace as we practice staying in the presence of God in prayer and supplication. Prayer will help us to focus on the Lord and the things of God. God wants to have true peace as we pray and meditate on His words. That means, we are thinking and meditating on holy things.

It is difficult not to have peace when you are thinking on pure and holy things. The things that are excellent and right in the eyes of God. Meditating on the words of God will transform us and renew our minds. Living is easy when we are transformed and our minds are renewed (Psalm 119:78). As our minds dwell on the things of God, we can make good decisions and live victorious lives. We can achieve peace when we practice the word of God. Psalm 16:11 tells us that God has made available to us the path of life filled with joy in His presence and eternal pleasures at His right hand. This life is free and makes living easy. As we continue to trust in Him, the God of peace will dwell with us.

Living is difficult when peace is limited or uncertain, but Christ gives us a peace that teaches, encourages and guides. Colossians 3:15 tells us that the peace of God calls us into one body and guides us into all truth. We are reminded in the scriptures that the peace of God is available in time trouble. The peace of the Lord surpasses all human understanding. Anxiety, worry and distress have a way of attacking us, but the Lord promises peace and encouragement. It is God's will that we live life to the fullest. Therefore, the Lord will bring calm to replace anxiety and relieve worry and stress in our lives.

The fruits of the spirit are love, peace and joy (Galatians 5:22). Its Jesus' intention for us to live in peace. He reminded us that we will have trouble, but He has overcome the world (John 16:33). We are encouraged to live in peace with all men if possible. He knew that people are difficult at times, and it would be an ordeal to live peacefully with them. Living is easy when we turn from evil, seek peace and pursue it (1 Peter 3:11). Jesus wants us to cast all our cares on Him. We are called to be peacemakers, to sow peace and reap a harvest of righteousness. The peace of God will guard our hearts and mind. It is important that we have peace because it promotes joy.

The Lord promises to bless His faithful servants with peace (Psalm 29:11). Living is easy when we love the laws of the Lord. This will bring us peace, and nothing will cause us to stumble. The word emphasized that the covenant of peace will never be removed from God's people because of His love for us (Isaiah 54:10). That is, we will go out in joy and be led in peace. Jesus said He gave and left peace with us. The world is not able to give us this peace; only God can. The kingdom of God is righteousness, peace and joy in the Holy Ghost. God is peace, He is the Lord of peace, hope and joy. In Him we live, move and have our being.

Living becomes difficult when we lack self-control. We need to be sympathetic and kind to each other. Believers dealing with unbelievers should remember that they were unbelievers at one time and Jesus redeemed us to Himself. It is our responsibility to tell others about the goodness of God. It not about us winning an argument, but our lives should be example of Godly living. As believers, we are expected to live in peace and harmony with self and others. We should approach people with meekness, kindness and love for each other.

Meekness is a fruit of the spirit, and we should all strive to develop this character of Christ. Living becomes easy when believers work to produce unity, peace and harmony. A meek person avoids envy, condemnation and strife because this is contrary to the will of God (James 3:13-18). James is encouraging us to practice love instead of hatred and malice. No one can experience peace where there is envy and strife. There is no place for envy in the presence of the Lord; therefore, if we dwell in the presence of the Lord, we will experience peace and hope.

Living is difficult when we cannot achieve peace or hope. Peace comes from Jesus Christ; He is the prince of peace and the giver of peace and life. Living is difficult when we live outside the will of God. Outside the will of God, we will experience unrest, distress and turmoil. There is no harmony without the peace of God. Harmony with the spirit of God will allow for the outpouring of the gifts of God: love, peace and joy in our lives daily. The kingdom of God is righteousness, peace and joy in the Holy Ghost. Even though we live in a world of trouble and discouragement, we can find peace in Jesus. Only Jesus can give us perfect peace and make living easy. Jesus is the inner peace.

He has given us victory over sin, sickness and disease, and this brings hope and peace. When we do things our way and according to our own understanding, we are acting against the Lord. Our ways are not in agreement with the spirit of Christ. Complaining, disagreeing and compromising will lead to sin and rebellion in our lives. In agreeing to the will of God, we are walking in His direction and purpose for our lives. Living according to the will and purposes of God will allow heaven to burst open and blessings to flow into our lives. According to Deuteronomy 2:7, it is the Lord that has blessed us with everything.

Living is hard when our spirit is not in harmony with the spirit of God, thus hindering the flow of blessings to us. According to Acts 2:1, on the day of Pentecost, everyone's spirits were in harmony with God's spirit. It was then that the Holy Spirit came as a mighty rushing wind and descended upon those who were in harmony with God. Those who stay in the presence of God will experience Him. They will eat the fruit of the land, and prosperity will be their portion.

The spirit of God cannot dwell in confusion because of His nature, neither can evil come close to His dwelling. Fear and disbelief will bring about disharmony in the life of a believer. A life without thanksgiving and honor to the Lord can never enjoy the presence of the Lord. Some of us murmur and complain about any and everything and forget it is the Lord who provides and protect us. We saw what happened to the children of Israel who were led by Moses in the wilderness.

Deuteronomy 2: 1-20 tells us that the children of Israel murmured ad rebelled in the wilderness. This led to their destruction because God was unable to pour out blessings because the people were ungrateful and disrespectful. Disharmony in our lives holds back the hand of God and His provision to us. The people did not fear the Lord and thanked Him for protection and provision. They were ungrateful and disrespectful to the Lord.

Disagreement with the principles of God leads to unfaithfulness and a sinful life. Unfaithfulness blocks the entry of harmony in the life of a believer. Lack of harmony prevents God from outpouring gifts and blessing upon our life. The children of Israel in the wilderness were unfaithful and ungrateful. They had forgotten all the miracles they had witnessed in the wilderness and, how God brought them out of Egypt. Their actions had blocked the glory of God from coming upon them. Obedience and gratitude will initiate the flow of Gods' blessing upon us.

There is absolutely no lack in the presence of God. To compromise is to rearrange our lives and to disconnect from the spirit of God. Compromise places us in awkward and terrible positions relating to the things of God. These positions are not only uncomfortable but also hinder the spirit of God from working in our lives. They block and hinder God's blessing in our lives. Compromise can cause living to be difficult and bring disappointment and dismay in times of trouble. God expects us to be transparent and live holy lives.

God is always sending His blessing, but we are the ones blocking them. When our spirit is in harmony with the spirit of God, heaven will burst open and blessings will begin to flow. Matthew 5:6 states that those who hunger and thirst after righteousness shall be filled. Therefore, we should delight ourselves in the Lord and wait for His blessing. We will be filled with goodness and favor when we obey the word and do the will of the Lord.

God's plan is for us to receive His rest (Hebrew 4:3). Those who walk in obedience will reap the benefit of rest. Rest is sometimes referred to as a person, place or personality. Every context of rest is meant for comfort and peace for those who trust in God. Living is hard when we do not have peace, feel lonely and hopeless. God is the one who grants us peace, grace, mercy and hope. The scriptures have made it clear that evil doers cannot enter His rest. Living is hard when we are caught in restless situation. The path of life is unpredictable, but God promised us rest protection and hope when we trust in Him. Faith is necessary for us to receive rest. Rest is harmony in the life of a believer. We cannot experience rest unless we in are harmony with the Holy Spirit.

Life is easy when we accept and receive the promise of rest. Those who are disobedient and fearful are unable to receive rest from the Lord. We need to ask God to purge us from filthiness and renew our minds daily. God is the creator and He rested after creation, so spiritual rest and physical rest are needed to live a healthy life. Living is easy when we receive God's rest; this will help us to live in confidence and trust the Lord more. We are promised renewal of our souls as we continue to do the things of God and learn of His goodness.

Testimony

I must confess that my best days are the days that I allowed the Holy Spirit to lead and control. I begin my mornings with prayer and worship to command my morning. On these days, I experience peace, joy and happiness. These are the days when I experience high energy levels and confidence. I go about my business with a smile, and no one can interrupt my mood or change my attitude. I just flow through the days without fear or intimidation. These are the days when I hear the voice of the Lord clearly, and I am more productive as I enjoy the presence of the Lord. The best part of our day should be early morning devotion: spending time with Jesus.

Chapter 3
CHANGES AND TRANSITION IN LIFE

Many people consider change to be a threat to their stability and often resist change. Others may view change as situation that can move them from a place of comfort and stability to an unknown or unfamiliar situation. This threat can create anxiety and fear of the unknown. We need to realize that change is inevitable in life, and though it may be necessary, not everyone will welcome it. The scriptures tell us that there is a time and a season for everything under the heavens (Ecclesiastes 3:1). So, we should expect change every day of our lives, and Jesus said He will never leave us or forsake us (Deuteronomy 31:8).

Transition or change requires preparation. Preparation is a process that many people fear; many people do not mind waiting but, it is what happens in waiting to be transitioned that may be uncomfortable creating suspense. Relaxing while we wait is not an option for the believer. In the preparatory phase, we need to hear God more because the enemy does not want us to cross over or transition if change will benefit us. Therefore, he is going to obstruct and resist. Joshua told the children of Israel to make preparation for crossing the River Jordan.

The preparation stage may mean to secure resources or supplies. As children of God, we should not be contented at the pre-crossover stage because the Lord has promised to take us to a better place. Joshua told the children of Israel that "in three days, they will cross the river Jordan to occupy the Land the Lord has given to them" (Joshua 1:11). Living becomes easy when we crossover to be at the place God wants us to be. The place God has prepared for us.

Living is easy when we listen to the Lord. He is always doing a new thing for us, making a new way (Isaiah 43:19). We have nothing to fear because the Lord Himself will go before us to make a way for us. Living is hard when we are unable to deal with change because we cannot control change. We are unable to control change and when we cannot adjust to change living is difficult. Change is real, and salvation requires change. The old must make way for the new as we go through repentance.

Therefore, change is necessary and important. According to Romans 12:2, we are cautioned not to be conformed to the world but be transformed by renewing of our minds to the perfect will of God. Change is needed to please the Lord. He does not change, but we are expected to change and grow spiritually in the ways of the Lord.

Personal

In my Christian walk, I have learned to welcome and appreciate change, especially when they are from God. I have learned that sometimes the Lord must remove some people from our lives who are preventing us from getting to the next level in our walk with Christ. It took me many years to realize that some people were fakers and would not be able to handle my spiritual success based on the gifts the Lord has given to me. It was very difficult for me to let go of several relationships, but as soon as I released those people who were never meant to remain in my life, I began to see the hand of God in my life. The Lord began to show me things and took me places I never imagined I would go. The changes became very real to me, and I welcomed them. The more I welcomed what the Lord was doing, the more I understood my purpose and began to experience a fulfilled life with the Lord. I began to appreciate the changes and some of the changes I wished I had taken earlier. Now, Jesus is all I want. He is the center of my life.

Seasons And Opportunities In Life

God work in seasons; He has set aside a time frame to bless His people. We cannot afford to miss our season or allow the doors of our season to close on us. In life, there are times of highs and lows, smooth and rocky. Regardless of what is going on in our lives, we cannot afford to quit because miracles happen in our season. Life is easy when we can recognize seasons and identify change in our lives. The inability to recognize the seasons in our lives can lead to disappointment and frustration.

Seasons are designed to produce change; many people are resistant to change and keep doing things the same way for years expecting a different result. This is unrealistic and may only lead to confusion and frustration. God has designed seasons to bless His children. Seasons are all about change; they come to improve our lives. God will help us to transition in our season. Living will become difficult if we resist change. Seasons are sent from God to provide either just enough or abundance. Whatever the case, it is controlled by God because He knows how much we need. Not enough always draws us closer to God; little is much when God is in it.

God has abundant blessings for His children, so we will have more than enough to sow seeds and bless others. Jesus has given bread to the eater and seeds to the sower. The seasons in our lives are either God sent or God allowed. The sources of seasons are: God, us, demonic and nature. Living becomes difficult when we try to dictate and control seasons. Sometimes the seasons change to bless us, but we often object to the very changes of the seasons that were designed to bless, either in rebellion or ignorance. God intends for us to have more than enough, but we sometimes miss the opportunity to receive the blessings. In God there is no limitations, it is men who limit themselves and others.

Nothing can surprise, God, he knows the beginning from the end. He has everything planned out for our lives. The enemy knows that God has plans for his children from the foundation of the world. The enemy understands seasons and change. He will do anything to manipulate and frustrate. His plan is to hinder the believer from receiving what God has in store for them. His intention is to create havoc in our lives hoping we will blame God for creating hard times. Sometimes when we are faced with difficulties and challenging situations, it is time to take an inventory of our life.

Examine our ways to see if we are walking in obedience. Disobedience can cause hardship and block our blessing. If we are in right standing with God, this may be an indication that our current situations are about to change for better, a season of blessing, a season of rain is about to take place. That is, the adversity we may be facing could be a distraction that the enemy designs to frustrate and confuse us to block our destiny. So, we need to ask God daily for wisdom, knowledge and understanding to make the appropriate decisions about life courses.

This can only come from reading the word, meditating on the word and building our faith in God. This is the time in our lives when we are most vulnerable and the choices we make will determine when and how we come out of these challenging times. Life is easy because God is faithful and He is still God. Success is not dependent on the duration of the battle but our attitude during and after battle. As children of God, we must remember that we are winners before, during and after battle.

We are all fighting from a place of victory. God has designed it that way, but the enemy of our souls would want us to believe otherwise. Life is easy when we can identify the seasons and opportunities that present themselves in our lives. The inability to discern the seasons in our lives can result in turmoil and disappointment. The Lord is good and is always making ways to prosper His children. Seasons are designed to create opportunities, to bless us and lead us into our destiny. As human beings, we are somewhat resistant to change, especially when we do not understand it. It is important that we do not miss these opportunities when they are presented to us.

If we continue to trust the Lord, He will show us these opportunities, and the Holy Spirit will prompt us to act. Taking the correct action will result in reaping the benefit of the opportunity given to us by the Lord. If we neglect to seek the Lord in every situation, we could make wrong decisions and miss opportunities. God has designed seasonal opportunity to bless His children. Even though seasons are about change, they come to improve our lives by bringing blessings. Living becomes difficult when we resist change and miss opportunities designed to bless us. Seasons are sent from God to provide either just enough or abundance, whatever the Lord decides. The Lord is faithful and knows exactly what we need and how much we need.

Not having enough will sometimes bring us closer to God. Little is much when God is in the equation because He knows how to multiply. God designs abundance so we will have more to sow seeds and bless others.

Sometimes the seasons change to bless us, but we often object to the very changes of the seasons that were designed to bless either in rebellion or ignorance. God intends for us to have more than enough, but we sometimes miss our or opportunity to receive the blessings. In God there are no limitations, it is men who limit themselves. Nothing surprises the Lord; He has everything planned out for our lives. The enemy knows Good's plan for his children from the foundation of the world.

The enemy understands season and change and will do everything to obstruct and hinder the believer from receiving what God has in store for them. The enemy is hoping that will remain in lack and struggle to succeed. The enemy believes that living in need will be the evidence that God does not care for those who say they belong to Him. Sometimes when we are faced with difficult and challenging situations, it is a sign that things are about to get better in our lives; a season of blessing, a season of rain is about to take place. That is, the adversity we may be facing at this time is a distraction from the enemy of what the Lord is about to do.

So, we need to ask God daily for wisdom, knowledge and understanding to make the appropriate decisions about life. This can only come from reading the word, meditating on the word and building our faith in God. This is the time in our lives when we are most vulnerable and the choices we make will determine when and how we come out of these challenging times. Life is easy because God is good and He is still God. It is not the length of the battle; it is the success or victory that counts.

As children of God, we must remember that we are winners before, during and after battle. God has designed it that way, but the enemy of our souls would want us to believe otherwise. Living can become challenging when we are unable to understand and recognize our seasons of blessing. According to Ecclesiastes Chapter 3, there is a time for everything under the sun. Everything thing that happens in the world does so at the authority of Christ. God controls time, season and harvest.

He requires of us to be sensitive to His voice, purpose and direction for our lives. God loves us so much and wants us to be able to access blessings and live successful lives. Therefore, we should be enthusiastic about the principles by which He operates. Solomon asked for wisdom, knowledge and an understanding heart. He realizes that these are necessary ingredients for success. God told Joshua that the secret for true success was to live by the book of the law and meditate on His words day and night. It is required of us to study God's word daily for insight and direction and to develop a close relationship with Him.

God sets the time for birth and the time for death. What are we supposed to do between these times? God himself controls time, and we all have this gift. Many people ask themselves, "What am I supposed to do during this time?" or "Will I have enough time to do what is required of me in the time allotted to me? "How much time we have on earth is a secret: only God know the time. So then, we must depend on Him for every direction and purpose. God is both giver of time and giver of life.

Changes And Transition In Life

Ecclesiastes 3:2 says there are a time for planting and a time for reaping. God is the one who gives us seed to plant (2 Corinthians 9:10); he gives seed to the sower. Life is easy because God is the keeper of our lives, and He is faithful and just.

God is a merciful God who takes care of His children. God is who He is; He does whatever He pleases. He causes rain to fall on the just and the unjust. God is perfect in all His ways. He gives us life, and He give us seed. What we do with the seed, or the prophecy will determine in part the magnitude of our success. There cannot be a harvest without sowing. The nature of the harvest is also dependent on the type of seed, nourishment and time of harvesting.

According to 2 Corinthians 9:6, "We will reap sparingly if we sow sparingly" Our attitude in sowing will determine the size and time of our blessing. When we think higher, we can achieve prosperity in the Lord. We should ask the Lord to send people into our lives who will help to foster our dreams. We all need mentors in our lives as we grow to teach, encourage and support us.

These people are equipped with knowledge and experience to do the job. Our life and living are complicated as well; therefore, we need directions and facilitation. Godly mentorship will allow us grow and mature in Christ. Living will be easy when we listen to the Holy Spirit and allow the right people into our lives. The Lord visited Sarah; He removed bareness and fulfilled the prophecy of childbearing. This was the visit she needs to remove the emptiness in her life because this had brought her embarrassment and shame. Living was made easy for Sarah because God removed bareness from her life and brought her joy and laughter. God is always working on our behalf to remove pain and suffering. We have also seen in the scriptures where God removed Hannah's bareness and gave her children (1 Samuel 2).

As we continue to turn away from our situation and look to Jesus in prayer and worship, He will rescue us. Jesus will remove all our pain and sorrow and replace them with joy and abundance (Exodus 4:31). Christ is the only one who can change seasons, break chains and bring abundant supply to our lives. God will never leave us to suffer. He loves us too much to fail us. We should wait on the Lord and allow Him to reveal Himself to us and change our situation. God's divine visitation brings provision (Ruth 1:6). Naomi went back to Bethlehem because she heard that the Lord had visited and the season of famine was over. She also had a visitation from the Lord, and her inheritance was restored.

There is a propitious moment for action: the moment when Lord show up that we cannot afford to miss: This is the time of refreshing, strength, power and deliverance. This is when a shifting of things occurs and the Lord sends blessings, healing, power, provision and anointing and prophecies are fulfilled in our lives As children of God, we need to live in His presence and expect Him to move (Jeremiah 29:10). As we continue to wait in His presence, He will send rain, and as we walk in obedience and cooperate with the Holy Spirit He delivers. Giving thanks to the Lord and waiting on Him will bring us joy and peace. We should not become weary in doing good because at the appropriate time, God will show up for us. We will reap a harvest if we do not give up.

Personal Testimony

I believe that I have missed out on some of these moments either because I did not know or did not use wisdom. I confess that in some instance, the wait seemed too long or I did not have the faith to believe who the Lord said I was. I have learned from my mistakes in my physical as well as my spiritual life. I have learned to identify and wait for my season: The Lord always showed up for me, and I was never disappointed. He has given me more than I ever asked for. I cannot afford to let my harvest go to waste or to someone else. The knowledge I now have of the Lord has helped me to understand the times and the seasons and to praise the Lord as I wait. All I want now is to stay in the presence of the Lord.

Sowing With Purpose

Even though challenging at times, sowing is possible if we trust the Lord. Many people tend to forget the principle of sowing and reaping. Living is difficult when people realize that if we continue to sow negative and false fruit, it is likely we will reap sorrow and negativity. Living is hard when we reap the negative things that we have sown in life. The word of God makes it clear that whatever a man sows, he will reap (Galatians 6:7)

In addition, we should not expect a harvest if we did not sow. We cannot have a harvest if we eat the seeds God has intended for us to sow. We eat these seeds sometimes because we are afraid, ignorant or disobedient. Not sowing for the future will not guarantee us a future harvest for generations to come. We are told in the word that "a good person leaves an inheritance for his children's children" (Proverbs 13:22). There is a season for everything under the sun; it is important that we make the preparation while there is seed and strength.

Living is difficult when we have missed opportunities during our lifetime and live to regret. Life is hard when we live without expectation because we have not sown for the future. Hard life brings negativity, regrets, disappointment and depression and frustration. On the other hand, sowing brings hope and happiness. Those who sow expect a harvest and have a positive outlook on life. Those who sow in tears will reap with joy (Psalm 126:5-6).

This is a great achievement for the sower. The sower develops a good attitude, makes plans for his future and sees life as being good and prosperous. God expects us to use wisdom and sow to reap abundance. He takes pleasure in our obedience to Him. It is the plan of God that we prosper and be in good health. We will be in good health when we sow. Our father in heaven is the one who controls the harvest. He will rebuke the devourer for our sakes (Malachi 3:11). We must ask the Lord to take care of our harvest, but we must do our part.

Sowing may be in the form of investment. Before investing in a project, a business or company, we should seek the Lord for direction. Often, we invest in unfruitful soil because we failed to seek the Lord for direction. This will lead to financial dilemmas and loss of substance. Sowing as the Lord directs will guarantee us a harvest and success. We must understand the principles of sowing: Jesus taught it is better to give than to receive (Acts 20:35), and God loves a cheerful giver (2 Corinthians 9:7). As we sow, we should expect a harvest; this is a great opportunity.

Testimony

One of the problems leading to divorce for many people is bad investments or poor financial management. Earlier in my Christian walk, I did not seek the Lord's guidance about these things because I did not know. At that time, I lacked the wisdom of how to handle finances and went along with what friends were telling me and the advice of other people. I later found out the hard way that we should not listen to friends but to the Holy Spirit. I sought the Lord after and He told me I was doing things backward––that is, after the fact. Now I asked the Lord first, I seek Him in every situation and He directs me. I have learned not to make impulsive purchases, decisions and agreements. Doing things God's way has brought me tremendous success. I sow in the work of the Lord where a harvest is guaranteed. I receive satisfaction from seeing people coming to the Lord and knowing Him. My giving to the Lord has helped feed the hungry and shelter the homeless. Making the Lord the center of my life gives me the satisfaction that God is in control. Now, everything is falling into place.

Chapter 4

Faith And Its Influence On Living

Faith may be defined as having complete trust in something or someone (Webster Dictionary). The spiritual meaning of faith according the word is: "the substance of things hoped for, the evidence of things not seen" (Hebrews 11:1). It is a connection power to God; He has become a tangible reality to the believer. We need faith to begin a relationship with God. Faith nourishes the heart and is just as important as the breath we breathe. Having that confidence in God and knowing that He is always there is very comforting for the believers. In other words, faith is the assurance that God is and that He is a rewarder of those who seek Him.

Living is easy when we place confidence in God. Disbelief concerning the things of God creates difficulties in our lives. Jesus cautioned us about disbelief; we must believe something. If we do not believe in God, then we believe in ourselves. The Bible mentioned several occasions where disbelief block miracles and leads to destruction. Faith is the precursor for miracles, and we cannot please God without faith. We learned through the scriptures the account of many miracles because of faith in God.

Disbelief blocks the flow of the Holy Spirit in our lives and locks us out of prosperity. According to Hebrew 11:6, It is impossible to please God without faith. Everyone who goes to God must believe that: He is a rewarder of them that diligently seek Him. Gods plan for our live is blessings and prosperity. Many of the challenges we face today are related to lack of faith. We would be able to move mountains only if we had a little faith: as small as a mustard seed. The currency in heaven is faith; we cannot do any transaction on earth without faith.

Lack of faith currency hinders success, miracles and blessings in the life of a Christian. Nothing will happen until we can touch the Lord: we touch him with our faith. In John 6:35, Jesus made it clear that he who comes to Him shall not hunger or thirst because He is the bread of life. Jesus reminded us many times that He is the bread of life. Living is hard when Jesus is not in our lives; we are not able to partake of the things He is and brings.

Living becomes unbearable when the children of God lose connection with the bread of life; that is, we have neglected the protector and the provider. We can show disbelief in life by turning to material things and education for satisfaction. Our faith will grow as we begin to understand and know the characters of God: His nature is good, kind and faithful. He is all that we need to live in this life and move.

A lack of faith will stifle our spiritual growth and hinder our prosperity. Disbelief will give the enemy access to bombard our minds with negative thoughts to further decrease our faith in difficult times. Disbelief will lock the door to all things pertaining to godliness as God has promised. That is, a person will be living and functioning at a lower level than God has intended for that individual because of disbelief. Sometimes there is a struggle between believing and doubting. This occurs when faith is not firmly rooted in the heart. We should not allow the enemy to play tricks with our minds.

We must take authority over our mind by renewing our minds daily and purpose in our hearts to believe Gods' word. Matthew 17:14-21 tells us that there was disbelief among the disciples that prevented them from casting out the demons from the possessed boy. So then, disbelief or lack of faith will hinder our success. Faith unlocks the hand of God to release blessing in our lives. God has given the believer all things pertaining to life and godliness. Faith is belief in God to do what He said He would do regardless of the circumstances.

Do not allow fear to direct your life because it will have a crippling effect on your life. Job said the thing I feared has come upon me (Job 3:25). I can recall how fear of closed spaced limited me over the years. I was afraid of elevators, close places and flying in an airplane. Then I heard a pastor said, "Your destiny lies behind the thing you fear." I started to seek God and asked Him to help me to overcome this fear. It took me over a year and today I must say God has come through for me. He told me I have no reason to fear because He never leaves. He gave the assurance in the scriptures.

If He never leaves me, then I am never alone. Living is difficult when we allow fear to cripple our lives. Fear is designed to keep us for reaching our potential and accomplishing what God has designed for us. Therefore, fear is a liar, and faith God's truth. (According to James 1:4-8) A double minded man is unstable in all that he does. He who doubts is like a wave of the sea and is blown and tossed by the wind. This person should not expect to receive anything from God. A person who doubts is double minded. In Matthew 6:24, Jesus stated that no man can serve two masters. He will either love one master or despise the other.

Living is difficult for the double minded because such a person will have conflict within himself. We often hear the term "a war inside." Such turmoil may lead to fear, restlessness, discouragement and depression. Hebrew 11:3 tells us that a double minded man has no faith. Faith is the confidence in what we hope for and the assurance in what we cannot see. So, by faith, we believe that God created the universe at his command. Our firm belief in God will bring stability to our lives. Stability will bring comfort and makes living easy because of our hope is in God. God rules in every area of our lives and in every situation.

The unstable mind cannot experience peace. Jesus Christ is the peace giver. God promises his people a peace that passes all human understanding. "And the peace of God that transcends all understanding will guard your hearts and your mind in Christ Jesus" (Philippians 4:7). The unstable mind is not able to comprehend or experience this peace. For such person, living is hard and does not make sense. On the other hand, the stable mind is able to think about what is true, what is pure, what is right, what is noble, what is lovely and what is admirable according to Philippians 4:8. The believer who experiences such thought pattern will live and experience God

Living will become easier because this person will be content in any and every situation according to Paul. The Lord blesses his people with peace (Psalm 29:11). To become an overcomer, God wants us to seek and pursue peace (Psalm 34:11). Life is easy because we can walk in the peace of God. 1 Thessalonians 5:23 tells us that God of peace will sanctify us thoroughly. The peace of God is available to us in every situation. We can have the peace of God in our homes, family, relationships, job, finances, health and even in storms that comes to us at various seasons and stages of our lives. The peace of God will bring resolution to conflict and hostility in our relationships.

Trust In God

Living becomes easy when you delight yourself in the Lord. Happiness is found in the Jesus. If we do this, we will never be miserable in our life. The Lord wants us to live in the joy of the Lord. Commit everything to the Lord, and Jesus will take care of our lives. Surrendering all to Jesus is giving Him everything. This is the key to life. Psalm 37:4 says, "Delight yourself in the Lord and He will give you the desires of you heart." So, the next time you think about worrying, how about delighting in the Lord. We were not made to worry. We were made to praise and worship the Lord and bring Him joy.

Life is full of trials and tribulations, but we are called to trust the Lord. If we give all our troubles to Jesus, He will see us through all our troubles. He can only do what we allow Him to do. Worry holds the hand of God from working in our lives. When we let go of the challenges and let God, suddenly the challenges will change to victory at the command of the Lord. The challenges in life remain challenges if we hold onto them. Jesus is the only one who can change trouble to blessings. Faith in God is believing His plan for our lives, His reason and timing. Storms and challenges come to strengthen us; the quicker we understand, the better for us. This is when life becomes easy because the Lord of glory is in charge.

The Lord commanded Joshua to be strong and courageous (Joshua 1:9). The Lord our God will be with us wherever we go. Proverbs 3:5-6 tells us to trust in the Lord and not in our own understanding. The Lord will make a way where there is no way. Isaiah 41:10 says we should not fear; the Lord will strengthen and care for us. In John 16:23, the Lord reminded us that the world is full of trouble but, He has already overcome the world. Peter told us to cast all our cares/concern on Him because he cares (Peter 5:7). The Lord reminded us that when we pass through the waters, we will not be swept away and, when we pass through the fire, we are not burned (Isa. 43:2). The flames of life will never overtake us if we put our trust in the Lord.

Testimony

The greatest thing in the world is to trust the Lord. There is a famous phrase "trust God and live, doubt God and die." I have adapted this as a motto for my life. Trusting the Lord daily is what brings me hope, joy and peace. This is what gives me the strength and assurance that God is real, and I see Him working in my life and working things out for my benefit. Sometimes the challenges are great, surmountable and difficult, but when I trust the Lord, He takes me through in ways that only He could. I depend on His guidance daily, and I am never disappointed. He helps me to solve difficult problems and gives me energy to face the day and get through difficult days. He gives me success in my job, favor and recognition. He is just an awesome and faithful God. He opens the Red Sea for me every day in my life. He told me He would provide, and He never fails to do so. He favors me on my job to retain my position. He tells me ahead of time what to expect, and I watch it happen.

Complaining And Its Effect On Living

Living is hard when we complain. Complaining means we do not trust the Lord. Complaining is like grumbling, and this irritates the Holy Spirit. According to Exodus 16:8, Moses told the people that they were not grumbling against him, but they were grumbling against God. Those who grumble do not know the Lord; therefore, the Lord is not able to work on their behalf. The people murmured in their tents and did not obey the voice of the Lord (Psalm 106:25). Paul encourages us to do everything without grumbling or questioning so that we can be blameless and innocent in the sight of the Lord.

Those who are crocked and twisted in their ways are the complainers and grumblers; their ways do not please the Lord. They question the ways of the Lord because they do not know Him. Living is easy when we hold fast to the word of God and trust Him regardless of the situation. The Word of God is life. Those who love the Lord will find peace and pleasure in Him. They will not grumble because they know that all things work together for good for those who know the Lord. A joyful heart brings healing. Those who grumble are selfish; they are concerned only about their pain and misfortune. They are preoccupied with their cravings and desires. They are ungrateful and proud; therefore, living is hard, and their labor is in vain (Jude 1:16).

Gratitude And Appreciation

Gratitude may be defined as a willingness to show appreciation and a readiness to show kindness. Living is easy when we learn to appreciate life and show kindness to others. A person can always tell whether their gifts are appreciated by the attitude and action of the receiver (Philippians 4:1-23). Paul expressed how grateful he was for the gifts and prayers of the brethren. He also gave detailed account of how the contribution was handled. It can be concluded from the conversation he had with the believers that he was a good steward of the fund.

His gesture of appreciation was genuine. The Lord expects us to be good stewards with our gifts and substance. God has given us the greatest sacrificial gift, the gift of salvation. The Lord expects us to be thankful and grateful even in difficult situations at all times. God has promised His grace and increase in faith during difficult situations. Living is hard when we are not grateful. The ungrateful person is unable to receive peace, hope and joy as promised in the scriptures.

Thanksgiving to God will allow a renewed mind with an overflow of grace. He promised us that His peace will reign in our hearts when we live a life of thanksgiving (Psalm 100: 1-5). Thanksgiving is one of the qualities we need to share the inheritance prepared for us. In hard times, the prayer of thanksgiving will bring hope. The more we give thanks; the more grace is available to us. This shows an attitude of returning kindness to God. This will help us to offer gratitude for our food, shelter and family every day no matter what the situation may look like.

Gratitude is also seen as good manners; it helps to boost relationship. That is, our emotional, physical and spiritual life is enhanced. We all need healthy mind and self-confidence as we learn to appreciate the things of God. This will help us to be in good standing with God the father. Being in good standing with Jesus affords us the privilege of asking for guidance and victories. The favor of thanksgiving will elevate to places of victory in Jesus. Favor of God reduces stress and anxiety. So then, when we thank the Lord, we experience peace and hope that relieve stress and anxiety. The result is emotional stability and sound mind. The joy that thanksgiving brings make us understand more of the peace of God and eager to share our experiences with others. We are then inclined to be witnessed for Christ and share our testimonies.

Chapter 5

Procrastination And Time Management

Living is difficult when we fail to realize that it is God who gives ability and opportunity. According to Exodus 31:1, "I have given him understanding, skill, and the ability for every kind of work." He has given us the ability to plan, develop and implement ideas and inventions. Procrastination is designed to delay our purpose, steal out time and delay our destiny. Many of us depend on people to provide sustenance, but the scriptures tell us that God is our provider. The sooner we realize this, the better life will be for us. In Philippians 4:19, we are told that "God will supply all our need according to His riches in glory in Christ Jesus."

According to Jeremiah 29:11, God said he knows the plan he has for us plans for our welfare and not for evil, plans to give a future and hope. Therefore, it behooves us to trust in the Lord in the Lord with all our hearts and lead not on our own understanding (Proverbs 3:5). We often procrastinate because we are fearful and lack understanding. Procrastination will provide temporary relief from anxiety. That is, it allows the individual to postpone a task for future time. Putting off a task for a future time may be unproductive, especially if we are not disciplined to follow up in a timely manner. This can cause us to miss opportunities and breakthroughs that we need to progress in life.

Opportunities are sometimes seasonal, or they may be in cycles. Seasons and cycles are related to time. God controls times, season and cycles. It is imperative for us to seize an opportunity and control cycles. The enemy understands cycles; we need the wisdom of God to change cycles. We cannot afford to miss the breakthrough we have been waiting for. We must be patient and diligent when waiting.

There are some tasks that we cannot afford to postpone in life. We need wisdom to decide which tasks or activities are too important to put off for another time. It is important to identify the tasks that are high priority and complete them first, then postpone those that are not as important. Lack of wisdom can cause us to misappropriate these tasks and mismanage them. We need to ask the Holy Spirit to help us to identify and rank our daily task correctly.

We also need the Lord to help us to break down and prioritize our tasks daily. Therefore, we must seek the Lord daily to help us to fulfill the important tasks in our lives. Failure to seek Lord may cause us to mismanage our daily tasks and miss opportunities. In Matthew 11:28, Jesus calls us to come with the burden and promises to give us rest. Therefore, we ought not to be prisoners of procrastination. The master controls the seasons and does not change.

Jesus is our all in all; we need not fear anything or anyone. As we continue to trust the leading and the direction of the Holy Spirit, we will find that all important tasks are timely and managed effectively. The Lord holds all wisdom and makes all thing new. We have no need to worry because the Lord controls all season. The Lord will order our steps as we continue to trust Him. We are tempted to procrastinate when we are unable to prioritize. Allowing the Lord to lead us daily will help us to organize and complete daily tasks. Living is easy when we can manage time, and complete important task that the Lord has given to us.

Living is hard when our lives are disorganized. Because of this disorganization, we tend to want to compete with the Holy Spirit and do what we think is best. That is, we may take on too many projects or assignments. If we are working on too many projects simultaneously, we will not be able to concentrate on anything that needs attention. Some things in our lives just need more attention than others. If we operate this way, it could be setting up ourselves for failure.

It may be beneficial for us to take on one project at a time rather than several simultaneously. We should seek the Lord about everything no matter how simple they may seem. We need the Lord to help us to make decision because He knows everything and what is best for us. He knows what we need before we even ask. We become overwhelmed when we plan too much in a short time and do not allow ourselves to rest. Tiredness will prevent us from achieving the best results. To get the best results, we are required to organize projects and assignments.

We all have the assignment to perform self-care, and this takes a good portion of our time. The Holy Spirit will help us to organize our activities and manage our time. Living is hard when we have poor time management skills and are unable to organize ourselves and our tasks. Organization will help us to eliminate clutter, do similar tasks together and manage our time effectively.

Living is easy when we can manage our time and balance our tasks. Guided by the Holy Spirit, we can prioritize activities and accomplish tasks timely and effectively giving God the honor. We must be realistic and be honest in all that we do. It is immoral to make promises we are unable to keep. There is nothing wrong to say upfront that there are tasks we will not be able to accomplish. As believers, we are held to a standard of integrity.

Living is hard when we are not able to manage our lives. Life is full of stressors and perceived stressors. As good stewards, we should be able to develop strategies to receive spiritual support that will enable us to handle and manage these stressors. We need to seek the Lord daily, let Him know our concerns and help us to organize our activities, solve our problems and resolve conflicts. We must give attention to what the Lord is saying and be committed to His leading.

Living is hard when we set unrealistic goals or selfish goals for our lives. This could be one reason for frustration and disappointment when goals are not attained. We must realize that all of us were created for a different purpose, and with different skills and abilities. Our goals should be the ones God has intended for us. If we want to know what those goals are, then we must consult with the creator. The one who created us knows us best. According to Jeremiah 1:5, the Lord told him that He knew him before he was conceived.

How can we know the mind of God and His purposes for our lives? There are many ways to find out this information. First, we must be able to hear the voice of God. He is always talking to us. He said in His word, my sheep knows my voice and another they will not follow (John 10:27). Mistakes will be made when we are unable to identify the voice of God in our lives before making decisions. God also speaks to us in visions and through His word. He has the blueprint and manuals for our lives. Living is hard when we live our lives using the blueprint of others. It is very unfortunate when we take counsel from the ungodly. Blessed is the man who do not take counsel from the ungodly (Psalm 1:1).

Living is hard when we make plans first and then consult God when our plans fail. We should consult God before we make plans to avoid failure, disappointment and shame. Living is easy when seek God before making plans, especially when these plans have the potential to impact our lives long-term. Proverbs tell us that many are the plans of men, but it is the Lord's plan that will prevail. It is important that we seek God's approval for our plans. We must realize that the choices we make have consequences. How we make choices should be dependent on what we know about our heavenly father. He is our creator and set a mandate for our lives. If we do not consult with Him prior to making choices, the result can be catastrophic in our lives. A difficult life is a hard life reality for many people. The appropriate thing to do in this circumstance would be to get God's approval. This requires faith and patience.

Testimony

I see procrastination as a stronghold. It was not until I started praying against procrastination that I was able to write this book and do other things. It took me six years but, I finally got a breakthrough. I have received testimonies from writers and songwriters about how they overcame procrastination. One of my mentors prayed with me several times to break procrastination, but I have learned that when God gives an assignment, the enemy plants procrastination as an obstruction to word or the prophecy on our life. The enemy deceived me, and I believed the time was not right. I found out it was a lie and started to destroy strongholds in my life. The enemy also made me feel that friends were supposed to help me; that too was a lie. I realized that I could do all things that the Lord has called me to do. So, with this knowledge, I called on the Lord, and He helped me to accomplish what He has for me to do.

Harvest And Timing

A harvest is a period for gathering. Those who sowed, planted or labored looked for a time of harvesting. Many people tend to forget the principle of sowing and reaping. Living is difficult when people realize they must reap the negative things they have sown in their lifetime. The word of God makes it clear that whatever a man sows, he will reap (Galatians 6:7). According to Genesis 8:22, the scripture tells us that if the earth remains, there is seedtime and harvest. God is the one gives us provision, and He can only do what we allow Him to do. He cannot provide for us if we do not believe he is a provider. He cannot protect us if we doubt, He is a protector.

Living is easy when we allow God to work in our lives. In difficult situations, we should learn to trust God. Some of the troubles we face were not meant destroy us; they were meant to make us stronger. We should appreciate the lessons learned from mistakes. Hardships do not come to destroy the child of God; they come to strengthen us. So, we ought to praise God during hardship because He is faithful. Living is easy when we totally submit our lives to our father in heaven. We must include God in our daily activities, as this lessens chaos and frustration in our lives.

God should be in our thoughts all the time, as we acknowledge Him in all that we do. We must honor God in the words we speak, the places we go, and the things we do (2Timothy 3:16). There are many lessons to be learned from Harvesting a harvest. The Lord is the who gives seed to the sower. The sower should expect a harvest. It is not unusual for those who did not sow seed to reap their desired harvest. We can only reap what we sow. It is dishonest and hypocritical to desire to reap what you did not sow. The scriptures have a lot to say about deception and dishonesty. A false balance is an abomination to the Lord (Proverbs 11:1).

Living is hard when people desire to reap what they did not sow. The eyes of the Lord see our heart; those who reap dishonestly will receive their portion of judgment from the Lord. Living is easy when we are honest with ourselves and others. The Lord wants us to live above reproach and be good stewards of what He has given us. Many factors can affect harvesting. If we are ignorant of these factors, the quality and quantity of our harvest may be jeopardized. We must know when to harvest––climate, temperature and season are factors to consider.

Timing is of utmost importance because we can reap either too early or too late. Reaping too late can lead to decay of crops. Decay may lead to poor quality products and decrease in value and quantity. Living is hard when we experience a decayed harvest. A decayed harvest can also lead to economic, emotional and spiritual decay. In the event of a spiritual decay, the individual may experience loss of zeal in their spiritual walk. This may lead to frustration and depression.

The inability to identify and discern our season for reaping can make living difficult for us. The plan of the enemy is to steal our harvest. The enemy takes delight in the destruction of our harvest in whatever way he can. Misinformation and lack of wisdom can affect our harvest. Listening to the advice of others can affect our ability to hear the Lord. We should only accept Godly counsel because only the counsel of the Lord will stand. Our goal should be to pay attention to the fruits of our labor and ask the Lord to help us to recognize the correct season for reaping.

Listening to the critics, using poor judgment or acting with selfish ambitions may result in missed opportunities. We should be able to recognize signs of growth and maturity. According to John 4:33, we should not say we have four months until harvest, but we should open our eyes to see that the fields are ripe for harvest. Living is easy when we can recognize the signs of harvest time.

Experience

I have learned from past experiences not to take cues from the critics, the negative, the weak and the ungodly. Lack of knowledge led me to act either prematurely or late and have suffered poor harvest. I listened to the critics and lost money in the stock market because I did not know when to buy or sell. I made decisions based on feelings and experience, but the Lord has taught me how to discern my harvest. Now, I no longer make the same mistakes, and if I am not sure, I ask the Lord. Jesus is the only one who knows the seasons to sow and reap.

Past Experiences And Mistakes: Effect On Living

Living is difficult when we are focused on the past. Life in the past may have been filled with disappointments, rejection, fear and oppression. This fixation on the past can hinder us from advancing to the future. Many of us we are still wondering how we made it thus far because of our horrible past, mistakes and failures. It is not by chance that we are here today delivered from the horrible place of disappointment, rejection, abuse, depression and oppression. It was God who delivered us, and He is still working on our behalf. Many of us were left for dead, still carrying wounds and scars from the past. The very thought of the past scares us.

The enemy knows that many of us fear our past and brings it back to remind us every opportunity he gets, but when the devil reminds us of our past life, we ought to remind him of his future. The enemy enjoys bringing up the script, but the Lord is the one who deletes it permanently. The enemy uses our track record to deter us from walking in our destiny. He does so in a way to distract us from the current preview of our life. Isaiah 43: 18-19 tells us not to cling on the events of the past or to dwell on what happened long ago.

Instead, we are to watch for the new thing God is doing and focus on the now. The Lord encourages us that our latter will be greater than the former. God is the one who makes a road in the wilderness and streams of water there. If we continue to dwell on the past, we will miss opportunities that are presenting themselves in the now and the future. God wants us to live in the now but, the devil wants us to live in our past.

If the enemy can get you to think about your past experiences for five minutes, your entire day will be ruined. Remembering the past will create doubt, frustration and even anger. To avoid such a dilemma, we must renew our minds daily. We must have a new mindset in the Lord. Romans 12:2 tell us not to conform to the things of the world but, we should let God transform our minds completely so we will know the will of God. Transformation comes with the daily renewing of our minds.

Living is hard when we make mistakes and are unable to let go of condemnation. Everyone has done or said something crazy or stupid in their lifetime. We are all imperfect and ignorant in many ways. Depending of the nature of the mess, many of us struggle to deal with it. This challenge often results in condemnation of various degrees. Condemnation can come from many people around us. We sometimes forget that God is merciful and has made unlimited grace available to us. Also, we should learn from our mistakes and use them as steppingstone to greater success.

We all face trials; the Word tells that trouble follows man, but the righteous escapes them. We should never allow mistakes and trials to become the challenge for spiritual growth (James 1:4). Living is hard when we allow trials and mistakes to stifle our spiritual growth because we lack wisdom and do not understand how important it is to exercise patience. He is a kind and loving God who will let us experience a meaningful life if we only trust Him. Life is easy when we depend on Him, when we trust Him, and acknowledge the power of the gift of grace and mercy. Most people like to have the manifestation of grace in their lives.

Grace conquers all our past failures and mistakes and is available when we need Him. Grace is a person, and his name is Jesus. God is love and will allow His love to shine through us if we trust in Him. Life is easy when we grow and mature in the grace of God. If we continue to focus on our problems and our mistakes, the problem or mistake will be magnified in our lives and the light of Christ will be obscured. As we magnify the problem, the way we perceive Jesus is diminished. Living becomes easy when we see God bigger than our problems. That is, we are giving the Lord permission to work in our lives.

God wants us to trust Him and depend on Him for life and sustenance. A trusting life will move the hand of God to do the miraculous in our lives. God is faithful and just to forgive us for our mistakes but, sometimes we cannot forgive ourselves. We are not our own and need to let go of the past to allow God to work in our lives. We cannot fix ourselves because we did create our self, so it is best to let God do the fixing. All we need do is to trust Him to care for us. He is the only one who can perfect and complete the process. The Lord is faithful and will complete what He has started. He is the creator and only He has the mold to recreate and transform us. Yielding to Christ is the best thing we can do in life.

He is the Alpha and the Omega and does not have to search for answers. He knows everything. He knows we were going to make the mistake before we did. He has already made plans to remedy the situation, the problems and the mistakes before there was even the thought. Jesus told Peter that he would deny Him three times before the cock crowed three times. He made preparation for Peter even before he denied Him. After His resurrection, He recognized Peter's weakness and sent him words of comfort. He is a kind and forgiving savior. Our mistakes do not cancel our destiny. Our best days are ahead of us because God is faithful.

Living is hard when we are brokenhearted. Jesus came to heal the brokenhearted. Many people have died from a broken heart. They unfortunately were unable to receive their healing or not knowing the healer. The challenges we face, the disappointments and missed opportunities and trouble can contribute to heartbreak. We have no control over these circumstances but trusting in God will help us, to be overcomers. Living is easy when we stand in the authority that God has given us. The word of God can help us to work out our problems as we allow God to use His power and work out our dilemma.

In 2 Corinthians 12:9, Jesus said that His grace is all we need because His power is greatest when we are weak. Therefore, in our brokenness grace is enough to heal our hearts and make us strong. In hardship and difficulties, Christ is there to help us. Psalm 147:3 says, He heals the broken hearted and binds up their wounds. Even though we are hurting and feel alone, God is with the broken. He sees the broken heart and will nurture until the heart is healed. Healing takes time, and we must trust the savior with our hearts.

Testimony

I struggled with the mistakes I made in my life for many years. They were like ropes around my neck. They haunted me day and night. Sometimes I felt like the Lord did not want anything to do with me. I was so depressed, and I did not laugh for over a year. At the time I was angry, oppressed and depressed until I had an encounter with the Lord. The Lord anointed me with laughter, and I have not stopped laughing since. Over the years, I have come to realize how much God loves me despite of the mistakes I have made. I am also able to help others to come to the realization that there are no boundaries or limit to the love of God. It was for these reason that Jesus died to redeem us from sin. Now that I am free from the bondages, I am happy and grateful for the love of God.

Chapter 6
WISDOM AND HEARING GOD

Following God's instructions is required to live a meaningful life. God's wisdom is what we need to be successful in life. It is imperative that we know God's plan for our lives. Living will become meaningful only when we know our purpose and recognize our importance on earth. Understanding purpose will allow us to be successful in life. Purpose is one factor that will help us, direct, and motive us to walk circumspectly.

A purpose-driven life, even though we may be faced with challenges, will stand the test of time when the focus is on God. Living in God's direction helps us to build confidence and courage. Fierce attacks from the enemy will not intimidate or deter us when we walk in the will of God. God wants us to prosper. The wisdom of God helps us to build good character. The intelligence that wisdom gives help us to grow and develop understanding, give good advice to others, love and respect them. The intelligence we receive will enable us to instruct the inexperienced and the vulnerable to live an honest life.

The skill of wisdom begins to develop from childhood and continues through life. It is the responsibility of parents to teach their children Godly principles for them to have a solid foundation. They should be taught to develop good qualities such as honesty, respect, humility and patience. Living is hard when we lack these qualities and live our lives with poor judgment.

Wisdom helps us to do good to others, help those who are in need and not causing harm to others. Our neighbors will trust us when our lives reflect these qualities. Many people are violent because they lack wisdom. They have rejected the Lord and are exposed to hidden disasters. The Lord hates those who do evil (Proverbs 3 :33-34). Living becomes easy when we love wisdom, get education and guard them well. Wisdom will prevent us from going where evil people are and follow their example (Proverbs 4:14).

Living is easy when we make wise choices daily by following the Lord's instruction. The Lord may use many channels to speak to us. He speaks to us directly or through His word. We must find time for the Lord. He is always speaking; we are required to listen attentively to His word and instruction. If we seek to know and fear the Lord, we will be successful in all that we do. The Lord gives knowledge and understanding as we seek Him. He protects those who are honest and righteous, those who respect and obey His commands.

Listening to the voice of God will allow us to do and say what is right. A knowledge of God will help us to know and understand our environment. This knowledge will help us to protect ourselves and live with integrity. People who live without wisdom find pleasure in evil and enjoy darkness. Because these people abandon righteousness, they are unreliable and cannot be trusted. Wisdom is the word of God appropriately applied to our lives daily. Accuracy and success in the activities of our daily lives requires God's wisdom (Proverbs 10:23-25).

Living is hard when we despise correction and disobey the teachings of the Holy Spirit. We must incline our ears to those who are ordained by the Holy Spirit to teach and instruct us. Often, we become hardheaded and self-advised. This leads to independence when we rely on our own thoughts and feelings to make decision rather than the instructions of the Lord. We are discouraged from listening to strange voices and familiar spirits. This is one avenue that the enemy uses to launch his attack on us. Listening to familiar spirits can lead to open doors in our lives for the enemy to unleash his attack. The scripture says, "My sheep know my voice and another they will not follow" (John 10:27).

If we listen to any other voice, we are tempted to embrace false teaching and incorrect information. Hosea 4:6 states, "My people are destroyed for lack of knowledge." Living is hard when we reject the knowledge of God because this will bring regret. Those who reject the teaching of the Lord rejects Him. The Lord knows the ways of man, the feet of the righteous is ordered by the Lord (Psalm 37:24). Walking in the way of the Lord will cause our fountains to be blessed. At all times, the Lord will protect, guide and sustain us when we put our trust in Him. We will not fall into traps and plots of the enemy.

Honoring the Lord will make us wise. He gives us sound instructions when we honor and obey Him. Happy are those who honor the Lord because He takes pleasure in them. The Lord will bless the descendants of those who honor the Lord (Psalm 110:10). He promises blessing and prosperity. Those who honor the Lord will never fail, and they will always be remembered as good persons. Also, they are not afraid of bad news because they trust in the Lord.

Therefore, God knows what is best for us according to His purpose for our lives. I have learned in my life that whenever I do something out of the will of God, I do not get good results. I have come to realize that God works by divine prompting of the heart, a heart that is not ready for such insight lacks spiritual guidance; hence, living becomes difficult. According to John 10:10, Christ came so we can live life to its fullest. We owe ourselves the joy and happiness provided by the Lord. We should seek out and take full advantage of these blessings.

We all need the wisdom of God: that is insight, intelligence, skill and prudence to live a successful life. The wisdom of God is the way we ought to live. As we engaged in actively seeking and living for God, we will realize that he takes pleasure in us. The knowledge and experience we gain will prove that the Lord is with us. He alone can guide us to making sound decisions. According to Proverbs 4:2, "I give you sound learning so do not forsake my teaching." This will help us to make wise decisions and thus making life and living less complicated. We have all we need in the Word to live a life of success.

God knows our future; regardless of the circumstance, all we need is to trust God. We must take his instructions for our life, a way of life. Sometimes He says yes; other times He says no. Waiting on the Lord is key to our success. He knows when the storm is coming, and when we obey, we are protected. Wisdom helps us to think, judge, distinguish and apply God's principle to our lives. Divine wisdom empowers us to prosper, conquer the enemy and develop Godly relationships.

Applying all these concepts to our lives helps us to be successful and living easy. A successful life requires divine counseling; God can never run out of ideas for our lives; he is giver of life and wisdom. Wisdom gives us the ability to see and plan––that is in accordance with the word. Living is hard when wisdom is lacking. Those who oppress others and disrespect the laws of God lack wisdom. People who disrespect others and their property have no knowledge of God. There are consequences for those who acts irresponsibly and without wisdom in their daily lives.

Many who lack wisdom are either imprisoned, fined or live to regret their actions due to lack of knowledge. Living is hard when you build your life on faulty foundations. Matthew 7:24-27 tells us that an unwise person builds his house on sand. A sandy foundation may be one that lacks faith and hope in Jesus. One that makes self the focus, material and earthly possession. A faulty foundation is one of wavering, uncertainty and fragility. Such foundation is unable to withstand the storms of life and pressures of life. We want to build our foundation on Christ Jesus where life is guaranteed. Jesus promised to be with us and take care of us if we put our trust in Him.

The wise man builds his house on the firm foundation. This foundation is Jesus. He is our rock and hiding place. The storms of life cannot destroy us if we make Christ the rock, the foundation in our lives. This foundation can withstand the pressure and storms of life. Jesus likened the doers of the word to a solid rock. Life is easy when we build our lives on Jesus and live by His words. Living is hard when we build on the foundation of fleshly desires and the influence of self and ungodly principles. A life based on selfish ambitions will become unsuccessful because we do not involve Jesus our father.

Living is hard when we depart from the ways of the Lord. According to Psalm 18:21, judgment will come when we depart from the ways of the Lord. We need to live so that our ways will please the Lord and not man or ourselves. As we begin to make our ways please the Lord and uphold His statutes, our lives will be more meaningful. It is the Lord who rewards His children according to His righteousness. We are rewarded according to the cleanliness of our hearts. He will be merciful to those who show mercy and upright to those who are upright (Psalm 18: 25-26).

Living is easy when we understand and live by the teaching of the Lord. Obedience brings prosperity to our lives. God is faithful to His children when we trust Him. We should not rely on our understanding and our way of doing things but rely on the Lord. Wisdom brings long life, wealth and honor to those who trust the Lord. Wisdom will cause our lives to be pleasant and safe. We will never stumble or afraid when we trust Him (Proverbs 3:13).

To hear the voice of God requires that we connect to Him. We connect to God through meditation, dedication and contemplation. The scriptures tell us that a broken spirit and a contrite heart He will not despise (Psalm 51:17). He can lift every burden, every weight and remove every difficulty. We can connect to Christ when we engage our minds, thoughts and emotion. We can do so by disconnecting from our fears and desires. He will reassure us when we go to Him with a grateful heart. Then, we will be connected to his faithfulness.

We will hear God when we read the Word in an interactive way. As we listen and interact with the Word, we will hear the reassuring voice of Christ. The Holy Spirit will bring us intellectual knowledge, wisdom and direction (Matthew 13: 11). This will strengthen and encourage us. Reading the Word with a deep concentration and having a conversation with God will draw us close to Him and make us better able to hear His voice.

The scriptures tell us that "My sheep hear my voice and I know them. They follow me" (John 10:27-30). As we clear our minds of worry and concern and focus on the scriptures, we will hear the Lord speak to us. It should be our desire to hear from the Lord daily. It is important that we read the Word of God daily and seek the Lord all the time. Moses went up to the mountain so he could hear from God.

Living requires that we hear from God all the time. Hearing from God will shape our thoughts, character and purpose. God can speak to us through His Word, vision and others. The voice of the Lord is governed by peace and love. His voice does not pressure, intimidate or create fear in us. There is a spiritual peace within when the Lord speaks, and even if there is turmoil around us. Only Christ can give that inner peace, that assurance and love.

As children of God, we must learn to recognize His voice, especially when making decisions. He may want us to wait in a situation, or He may say go ahead. The Lord is not bound by time or in time. The pressuring voice is the enemy who wants us to make wrong and costly decisions. The enemy pressures and intimidates us, always putting time limitation and deadlines. The intention is to drive us to act in fear. Living is easy when we recognize the devil's strategies and avoid his traps and snares.

The Effects Of Obedience On Living

Obedience is superior to understanding. Obedience requires commitment and consistency. Commitment requires stability and excellence. Obeying God's word brings excellence and stability in our lives. We need to include God in our daily lives so we can have the anointment of ease and rest that only the Lord can give. This approval helps to relieve frustration and remove chaos and disappointment. Disappointments and sadness can lead to discouragement and depression.

Obedience to God will result in His favor in our lives. The favor of God at work in our lives brings courage and strength. The bible says believers are called to a life of obedience. This involves hearing and harkening to God's authority that is the greatest there is, God is the supreme power (John 14:15). Life can become a real challenge when we walk in disobedience. The word of God is like a mirror that directs us through life.

Disobedience is like seeing the imperfection in the mirror and ignores it, hoping it will take care of itself. Unfortunately, that is how some of us live and often ask ourselves why life is so unfair. Disobedience is a sin that can lead to destruction. Obedience flows from a grateful heart, and God rewards obedience (Genesis 22:18). It is associated with blessings and prosperity. Therefore, let us be honest to ourselves, and the next time life throws a curve ball at us, let us examine our walk.

Because God rewards obedience, could it be we were disobedient? Or did we leave the flaws unaddressed the last time we look in the mirror? Sometimes, it is very frightening to think that we create problems for ourselves when we disobey God. God blessed Abraham because of his obedience. Exodus 19:5 says, "If you obey me and keep my commandment you will be my own special treasure from among all the people from the earth." If we want to live a life of abundance and prosperity we must walk in obedience. Disobedience is walking contrary to the will of God. The Lord promises to send plagues on those who walk contrary to His will (Leviticus 26:21). Also, those who walk contrary to God's will steps into error and destruction.

The Lord calls those who walk contrary to His word as being wicked (Deuteronomy 9:5). Those who continue to walk contrary even after they were corrected are considered as enemies of God. The ones who willfully walk in disobedience are considered shameful and disgusting in the eyes of the Lord. They do not have the favor of God in their lives; ultimately, life is hard for them. Obedience to God is a form of demonstrating to Him that we trust and believe Him. Through obedience we experience the blessings of life and living is made easy. Joyful are the people who follow God's instruction on living, His laws and walk in His path (Psalm 119: 1-8).

There are several blessings attached to walking in obedience to the will of God. Obedience comes with the blessing of favor and abundance. Those who are obedient will be fruitful and live a prosperous life. Living is easy because the obedient person will see the destruction of their enemies and live victoriously (Deuteronomy 28:15-30). The promise states, "If we obey the Lord, we will be the head and not the tail, above and not beneath." Living is easy as we will become the lender to nations. Living an obedient life is a prosperous life according to the scriptures.

Living is hard when people engage in disobedience concerning the commandments of godly living. The same way obedience is linked to blessings, disobedience is linked to curses. The scriptures tell us that there are consequences for walking in disobedience. Deuteronomy explains how disobedience brings curses on the land as a form of punishment. This punishment could be in the form of diseases, distress and disasters on the land. The curse may also lead to the destruction of vegetation by worms and locust. Disobedience cost Adam and Eve the Garden of Eden and their connection with God.

Famine was be a direct result of a cursed land to those who experienced this. Curses may also result in self destruction and bondages for generations to come. The Lord is wonderful in all He does and all His commands are dependable. He promised to bless those who obey His commandments. Living is easy when we honor the Lord. He promised us a blessed and prosperous life. We are told in Proverbs 22:4 that if we obey the Lord and remain humble, we will receive riches, honor and long life. Disobedience leads to death and destruction.

Testimony

My life was miserable and unhappy because I was not living for God. I have seen the impact of salvation in the life of a brother firsthand. Disobedience had brought him much heartache and loss--even his health was threatened. The moment he gave his life to the Lord, he was renewed. He continued to trust the Lord and believed. He was miraculously healed from a cyst near his jugular: That cyst disappeared suddenly. This was a scary situation for all of us. We sought the Lord in prayer and fasting. I have never seen someone with so much faith. The doctors were scared and afraid to do surgery except as a last resort.

The young man went through several radiologic aspiration of fluid from the sac near his jugular. The procedure left him swollen and in pain, and he had to wear a lead vest for 1 week after the procedure. Two weeks later, the sac was again filled with fluid, and the doctors decided to operate because the cyst was putting pressure on the jugular vein. By this time, there was a large mass on his neck. The Lord miraculously dissolved the mass 1 hour before surgery. The nurses prepped him for surgery, the surgeon arrived with X-ray results and went to verify the location for surgery and could not find the cyst. The Lord came through for him, and we all celebrated the Lord for His goodness. God has again proven to be a healer and a deliverer. It has been four years, and there is no evidence of a cyst.

Chapter 7
Knowing Our Purpose And Identity

Every person needs to discover their identity and purpose in life. Knowing your purpose allows you to walk in your destiny. Not knowing your purpose may lead to frustration, disappointment and anxiety. God determines our purpose in life. The Lord will bring to pass whatever our purpose is in life. He sometimes reveals our purpose through divine encounter and direction.

At other times, He may use inward prompting; on other occasions, he uses visions and divine pictures. Sometimes we assign ourselves tasks or place ourselves in situations that drains us of our energy and at other times place excess strain on our bodies. Chances are the activity did not come from God; we often meet resistance when we try to do things God does not approve. So, we need to use wisdom in making decision. Exercising wisdom will help us to make wise decisions based on experience and Gods word. Even though situations may be challenging, the Lord will lead us to make the correct decision.

At times, our minds are bombarded with thoughts; this is the time we need to pray and ask God to help us to make the correct decision. In dire situations, we cannot make decisions without speaking to the Lord. Jesus said, "He is the way the truth and the life" (John 14:6). This goes to show again that life is a gift from God, an undeserving gift that should be appreciated and cherished. It is not a good idea to live without purpose or direction. A life without direction is not worth trying because it may lead to destruction.

God has predestined our purpose in life; therefore, we must wait on Him to get direction. He knows when we were going to be born and when life on earth expires. According to Habakkuk 2:2-3, when God gives us a vision, He wants us to speak the vision and more importantly write it down. We need to wait because it will come to pass. We cannot do things on our own, God must guide us continually and lead us through this life. God has us in the palm of His hand; He will take us where He wants us to go. He is working continuously in our lives when we let Him.

God has called us to His purpose. He knew us before we were born, and He has predestined us to be confirmed to the image of Jesus Christ, the firstborn. Living is easy because He has predestined us and justified us. If Christ had not died for us, we would still be in bondage. He has given us His everlasting love and, if God if for us, then who can be against us. Who then can bring charge against God's selected or chosen one? Therefore, life is free, and living is easy. All we must do is to encourage each other and reap the benefits of salvation.

Testimony

I never knew what my purpose in life was, but I knew I enjoyed telling people about the Lord. I enjoyed praying for people and encouraging them in difficult times. So, people would call me to pray with them, and I would pray to the Lord fervently. My passion for prayer grew, and I saw that the people I was praying for getting delivered and their prayers answered. The people who I witnessed to would give their lives to the Lord. I started a prayer group in my home, and the Lord did many miracles, people from week to week would come back with testimonies of breakthrough. They were also inviting other people. We worshiped and prayed until we received victory and breakthrough. My life is now prayer and worship. The hand of God is on my life; He did many miracles in my life.

Dreams, Visions And Talents

Dreams and visions are important to us. They are part of our growing up as we think about what we want to achieve: education, career, and occupation. Our dreams were based on the effect of our environment, beliefs and values. As we become more mature in life, our dreams change as well as our values. The Lord is the owner of our dreams, visions and talents. Therefore, only the Lord knows to manage them. As an owner, He gives and take away.

God has designed us with specific gifts, talents, skill sets and intellectual abilities. We were all born with purpose and destiny. Dreams are designed to connect us to our destiny, but God controls our destiny. We were created with potentials and emotions, but God directs our destiny. Each of us has a destiny and cannot fulfil another person's destiny. We were all born with inherent traits; when they are nurtured, they manifest at different stages of our lives.

Our dreams in life are the things we hope to aspire or they may be an expression of our ambitions. Living becomes difficult when we try to accomplish for ourselves someone else's aspiration or ambition. We are unique as human beings and created by God for different purposes. Therefore, each person has their own values, beliefs and dreams. We all have different talents, skill sets, intellectual abilities, and talents, we are expected to dream differently.

The scriptures outlined how we should live concerning dreams and goals (2 Chronicles 5:17). We are told to be strong and not give up because the Lord Himself will reward us. It is the Lord who gives us the desire to dream and make our plans succeed (Psalm 33:11). The plans of the Lord concerning us lasts forever. We must surrender all our dreams and plans to the Lord to make living easy. Only the plans of the Lord will prevail.

Living is hard when we have too many dreams, have not surrendered them to God and try to figure them out ourselves. Some people try to chase dreams and go after vanity seeking satisfaction. The scriptures tell us to seek first the kingdom of God and all other things will be added (Matthew 6:33). A heart that is focused on the things of the world cannot please God. The Lord wants us to be prosperous as we use our gifts and talents to please Him. He will allow us to achieve the goals and visions that will bring Him glory. Success will come when we allow the Lord to be part of our plans and celebrate His faithfulness with our dreams, talents and visions.

These dreams are supposed to empower and connect us with destiny. Everyone has different potential: God has created us with enough grace to fulfill the tasks He assigns us. We were called to be imitators of God and not man. It is not possible for us to try to live another person's vision for our life. This will only lead to frustration and eventually failure. We are supposed to give thanks to the Lord who gives the power to get wealth. The wealth belongs to the Lord, and the way we handle it should please Him.

Frustration due to failure or loss may lead to discouragement. Discouragement makes life difficult. We were made to have dreams and aspirations and maximize our potential based on the abilities given to us. Life can be beautiful if we understand who we are in Christ. He wants us to be productive and live a life of prosperity but, more so, he wants us to use the gifts and talents to please Him.

Living can be hard when you neglect to please God with your dreams, visions and talents. We are called to be good stewards with the gifts and talents God has given us. Our talent will help us to aspire and dream, but God controls their manifestation. The Lord is the one who allows us to dream. Therefore, we need to take our dreams to the Lord in prayer to get His approval. He wants our dreams to celebrate His faithfulness bring Him glory.

Knowing Our Purpose And Identity

Talents are free gifts from God; living becomes difficult when we bury our talents. A buried talent is a waste of wealth and investment. Persons who waste their gifts and talents have regrets later in life. Many found themselves in a state of ingratitude. This will only lead to frustration and eventually failure. We are supposed to give thanks to the Lord who gives the power to get wealth. Many of us are given talents to create wealth by investing. Talents are meant to empower us financially and emotionally. We are encouraged to help the poor and bless the work of the Lord.

The scriptures tell us that that Jesus was disappointed with the servant who buried his talent and praised the servants who invested on their talents and generated profits. We owe it to ourselves and our families to live a profitable life that pleases God. To be happy in life, we must be who God has created us to be. It is proper to admire positive things, gestures and the fine things of life, but we must always remember God is the creator, and He has the blueprint and manual for our lives. He is the one who has placed within us potentials.

According to Daniel 2:46-49, you're gifting will also bring you before great men. You do not have to settle with the world's standard. Everyone was created by God with a gift. The gift is what helps you to dream and have vision, goals and purpose for your life. Our gift is loaded with power, influence, it is magnetic in the sense that it either attract or repel.

Your talent can either bring people to you or push them away from you. God uses our talents for His purpose. Daniel's gift as a dreamer placed him in the king's palace, and Joseph's gift as a dreamer placed him in the king's palace as a prime minister. Our gift inspires other people and leads us to the right contacts, right time in the right season. Our gifts open door of opportunities and closes doors of failure and frustration.

Our gifts are loaded with rights: right time, right place, right people and right situation. The world has a need for everyone's gift; if the gift is not discovered and activated, then the world loses out and the individual may be labeled as lazy and good for nothing. A talent that is hidden is useless; a gift that is suppressed is dormant and unproductive. Failure to maximize our talents and gifts is irresponsible. This also show irresponsibility for our lives, lack of stewardship and unfaithfulness

One who wastes talent would have lost both worlds and ultimately live a miserable life. Many people are living today without hope because they have not unlocked that treasure "gift" given by God. Some have unwrapped their gift but lack motivation and wisdom to activate it. Yet there are others who procrastinate and find excuses as to why the gift is not activated. Sadly, for many people, they die before opening, activating or even acknowledging their gift. Life is easy when you can unlock and utilize your gifts maximally. This will help you to live your dream and live the life you deserve. God wants us to live our lives to the highest potential guided by Him. I am sure that at least 50 percent of us know or know of someone who is gifted and is yet to acknowledge the gift they have. Many people are envious of the talent or gift of others but, fail to activate their own gift.

A gift that is not activated is useless to the individual. There are struggling financially and emotionally because they are too lazy to use their gifts. Instead, they will ask another person who has been using their gift for favors and support. They are forfeiting a prosperous life to settle for crumbs. Many of us can become mentors for young people by helping them to discover and operate in their gift to glorify God. God has given us gifts and talents to glorify Him.

Chapter 8

HUMILITY AND RESPECT

Living becomes hard when we lack humility and are prideful. The Bible warns us about pride, arrogance, ego, self-exaltation, haughtiness and self-will. In Numbers 12:3, we saw how meek Moses was and how God used him as a result of his meekness. In Matthew 5:5, "Jesus said the meek will inherit the earth." He declared happiness to the meek. In Galatians 5:22-23, meekness is a fruit of the spirit. Proverbs 16:18-19 tells us that pride goes before destruction and a haughty spirit before a fall.

To avoid a difficult life, we must be led by the spirit to be happy. Meekness is an attitude of the heart; self-will is not approved by God; only His will counts. A humble person is concerned about the things of God. Humility do not mean weakness; it signifies strength as the individual depends on God. A humble person understands the nature and will of God and is ready to submit. Submission to God's word makes living easy. A humble person focuses on the needs of others and not on themselves.

The quality or attitude of the mind should allow us to depend on God. Humility helps us to realize our sinful nature and relies totally on God for sustenance (Acts 20:19). Living becomes easy when we acknowledge our vulnerability and weakness. We believe God for food, clothing and shelter. God requires a total dependence from the believer. Our humility towards God is a sign that we need Him, trust Him and appreciate Him. Therefore, it is not difficult to give God all the glory due to His name. Because we are weak, we tend to err; our dependence on God will cause Him to give us strength in our weakness, power and wisdom.

According to James 1:21-25, God requires us to put away filth, wickedness: He also wants us to become doers and hearers of the word. God's will for our lives should be first; this is living God's way. We cannot solve life's challenges alone, we need God. We would become frustrated, discouraged, and tired if we tried. We can only gain victory with God by our side. The enemy does not want us to succeed, hoping to cast doubt on the goodness of God in our lives.

The enemy will oppose everything we stand for in God. Doing things in our strength is a delight of the enemy because he knows we are incapable. He does not want us to succeed. This is a plot of the enemy. The truth is we cannot live without God; He created us with a void He alone can fill. We must follow His divine leading and He will guide us with his powerful hands. We must realize that God will do only what we allow him to do, when we doubt, He is unable come through for us. The enemy works very hard for us to doubt God; but when we act in His faith, we give Him the opportunity to do wonders in our life.

Living is easy when we realize that we can do all things through Christ. He is the one who gives us the ability. The victory is ours when we trust Him. As we humble ourselves before Him and trust Him, we give Him the opportunity to do the miraculous. The more we honor God, speak His words and trust Him, the more we experience Him in our lives (2 Timothy 3:16).

A meek and a humble person is not afraid to give honor to those who earn it. We are not allowed to belittle others to gain glory and recognition for ourselves. According to Romans 12:3, we should not think more highly of ourselves than we should but think soberly. We should not think we are more capable than others or have better ideas than

Humility And Respect

others. We must admit our weaknesses, and our deficiencies. No one is more deserving than the other when it comes to eternal life.

Anyone who practices these things will experience difficult living. We all need to appreciate the good qualities of others, as we all have different abilities and gifts. We must always give thanks to God for the good qualities that are in us. Romans 12:15 encourages us to rejoice with others when they rejoice and cry when others cry. Living becomes easy when we do these things God expects of us.

According to 1 Peter 2:17, we are called to show proper respect to everyone, love the family of believers and fear God. This will honor Jesus, and life will be easy as we live to please Him. In everything, do unto others as we would like them to do to us. Life is easy when we respect others; this is in obedience to the law and the prophet. We should be devoted to one another and honor others above ourselves. God has created everyone; we must respect them regardless of our perceptions. We should do nothing out of selfishness but be humble and respectful.

We should live by example, do what is good and show integrity. Only then will life be meaningful and living will become easy. We are commanded to love one another as Christ has loved us so others will know we are His disciples (John 13:34-35). Christ expects us to subject ourselves to governing authorities. God is the one who establishes authority. Living is hard when we rebel against God's authority. Those who do so will bring judgment upon themselves. The disobedient will be terrorized by the ruler; those who do right are free from fear. The servants of the Lord are agents of wrath who can bring punishment to the wrong doer (Romans 13:1-7). We should respect them.

Living is easy when we submit to authority and respect the authority of God's word. This is a matter of conscience and principle put in place by the Lord. We should hold in high esteem those who work in the kingdom. We are encouraged by Paul to love and respect them and live in peace with them. It is good to remember our leaders who share the word of God with us, show them regard and love them. Children are called to love and respect their parents, the first commandment with a promise of long life.

In todays world, we see how people handle authority. There are children who disobey and even destroy their parents. Many of the homes in society are without an authority figure and there is either role revision or role confusion. God gave authority for us to be in order, grow and succeed. On our jobs we have managers and leaders. We can be terminated or reprimanded if we disobey instruction. There are laws governing the land, if we disobey them there are penalties associated with these laws. Similarly, there are laws of God that if we disobey, we will face consequences. We should teach our children to respect self and others.

The Effect Of Favor On Living

Living is easy when the favor of God is on your life. Whatever situation you are in, God's hand is on your life. The favor of God can show up in unexpected ways that we cannot understand. The favor of God will show up in places we never dreamed it could happen. In addition, God's favor will show up in strange circumstances and situations. God's favor was on David in the field when Samuel anointed him. God is working behind the scenes and in our lives. Gods favor was in the pit and the prison with Joseph. He never understood that God favor was in the pit and the prison.

Joseph's father was devastated and grief stricken amid favor, but it would take the negative event of a famine for them to realize the favor of God in their lives. It was then that they realized that the hand of God was working even when they thought it was over. Joseph's brothers did not realize that they were creating the atmosphere for God to work. The scriptures say, "all things work together for good to them that love the Lord" (Romans 8:28). Joseph's brothers taught they had gotten rid of Joseph when they sold him into slavery. Joseph himself could not see the hand of God in his life; he asked the butler to remember him when he gets out of prison. God made Joseph the prime minister of Egypt.

Living is hard when God's hand is not on your life. There are many reasons for the hand of God not to be on your life. We can block the hand of God from our lives by sinning. Instead of letting God control our lives, we can block his hand by trying to solve our problems instead of allowing God. Those who believe in their own strength do not need God. The proud and arrogant will not see the hand of God. The flesh is selfish and self-seeking and cannot experience the favor of God. God will defend those who trust in Him and pleases Him. He will be their strength and shield in times of trouble.

How Faithfulness And Consistency Affect Our Lives

Faithfulness may be defined as loyalty, devoted and true hearted to the will of God. God wants us to bind ourselves to faithfulness so that we can find goodness and favor with Him (Proverbs 3: 3-14). If we are faithful to God, He will be faithful to us because that is His character and he cannot deprive Himself (2 Timothy 2:13). Living is easy when we are faithful to God and in the things of God. Those who are faithful to the Lord will reap many benefits. The Lord promises to promote our success, and His blessings will overtake those who obey (Deuteronomy 28:2). Christ will hold at a high standard those who are faithful and trustworthy (1 Corinthians 4:2). If we remain faithful, we will reap the good God has promised us. The Lord told Jeremiah that His plan is to prosper him and give him hope.

Living is hard when people becomes hopeless. Unfaithfulness can lead poverty and hopelessness. We require trust to serve the Lord because sin will sentence us to death. He cannot bless us if He can't trust us. We limit ourselves when we do not trust the Lord. Living is hard when we do not serve the Lord with joy and gladness. The Lord will allow those who do not serve Him to serve the enemy. Those who serve the enemy will become hungry and naked.

As children of God, we are called to be steadfast and unmovable always (1Corinthians 15:28). It is required that our walk is consistent with Christ. We are instructed to abide in Christ so that we can bear fruits. This means continued fellowship with our Lord Jesus. People of God are expected to pray and meditate in the word consistently. We should not be tired of doing good because we will reap a harvest. Consistency requires time and commitment. It is impossible to drink from the cup of the Lord and at the same time drink from the cup of the devil. We cannot serve two masters; we will love one or hate the other. As children of God, Christ must be the focus because He is the only way.

Consistency in our walk with Christ should be the goal of every believer. This will help us to grow deeper and stronger in the Lord. This will also increase our faith in Him, provides us with spiritual, physical and mental strength that we need every day. Consistency will produce joy and confidence in Christ. A confident walk with Christ will increase strength and momentum, leading to victory and deliverance. Deliverance came when the people of Nineveh fasted and prayed consistently. The Lord heard their cry of repentance and saved them. Therefore, consistency in the Lord guarantees success. Faithfulness, godly habits, thankfulness and obedience put us in good standing with the Lord (1 Corinthians 4:12).

Living becomes easy when we work hard on being consistent through struggles, We are encouraged to move away from our past and focus on the things of God. A focus on heavenly things will increase our growth spiritually, physically and emotionally. Our relationship with Christ is only genuine when we are consistent. The Lord will manifest Himself in our lives when we become consistent. We should be determined every day we wake up to please God in what we do or say. We should live a life that illustrates the goodness of God and His everlasting love for us.

We need to always remember that the enemy's plan is to distract, oppose and obstruct us so we become inconsistent in our walk with Christ. Therefore, we must remain focused and consistent in our walk. By being consistent in developing Godly habits, asking the Lord to transform us, will make us victorious over the enemy.

Humility And Respect

Living is hard when become self-centered. The scriptures teach us to be more concerned about the burden of others than ourselves. Romans 15 instructed us to help others to carry their burden. The scriptures instruct us to help others and be patient with them. Jesus took our place and He who had no sin took on our sin. Giving to a child of God is like lending to God and the scriptures say He will repay.

Encouraging others makes room for happiness, builds and strengthens us. Jesus took all our reproaches and abuses to make us free. There is a reward for those of us who are willing to love and encourage each other. Encouragement helps to build patience and endurance. Jesus is our hope and joy; His power enables us to be overcomers and hopeful in life. Living is easy when His love bubbles in us and hope runs over. As we consecrate our lives to Him, stay in His presence and exalt Him in our lives we will become successful in life.

He said when we do His will, we will lack nothing. As we continue to receive and welcome each other, sacrifice ourselves, hope, peace and joy will shine through us. The Lord will refresh us as we sacrifice for others to serve Him. The things that we make happen for others, God will make happen for us.

Chapter 9

ANGER

Peace of mind is what everyone desires. People want to live lives free of worry and care for their families. They also want to enjoy family, friends, jobs, work and church. No one desires to be burdened down. People who cannot find peace get angry and sometimes lash out against people and even God. Living can be difficult when uncontrolled anger is present. Anger can destroy relationships and paralyze communications. The Bible has much to say about anger. Everyone struggles with some degree of anger. God has made provision in His word for us to deal with anger.

James 1:20 tells us that anger could stem from pride. This anger may be sinful and those involved may experience the inability to step into the blessings God has promised. Anger is difficult to deal with sometimes because many people feel it is justifiable. This idea is either because we fail to take responsibility for our actions or just simply finding an excuse for inappropriate behavior. In 1 Corinthians 10:31, we are warned about prolonged anger.

Anger that lingers for whatever reason will become sin. Any sin in the life of a believer is danger and could result in the enemy attacking the individual. The angry person may not be able to pray fervently, sensing the prompting of the Holy Spirit or hear God speaking. A life without direction leads to confusion and frustration. The problem may become worse as the frustrated person could become violent and lose heart (Ephesians 4:26-27). Uncontrolled anger could lead to holding grudges and bitterness (Ephesians 4:26-27). It would be in the best interest of this individual to repent and show love to the supposedly offender. Living can be extremely difficult for this individual (Proverbs 29:11).

As believers, we must learn to control anger so that the peace of God may reign in our lives. According to Psalm 37:8, the Lord wants us to stay away from anger and not to fret, as this will lead to evil. A life of sin is a destructive one. Consequently, a life without anger is a blessed life. The meek shall inherit the earth and live in abundance. Do not let anger draws us into sin. Get rid of passion, anger and bitterness. We should not shout at people and hurl insults at them. The Lord wants us to forgive others as He has forgiven us.

Testimony

I had a problem with anger as a teenager: I was raised in a dysfunctional home. I was abused physically and emotionally. I was also in and out of difficult relationships and found myself to be a single mother of two early in life. I was angry at the world and wondered what I had done to deserve any of what was happening to me. I was saved at the age of 15 but fell out of fellowship with Christ. I thought God was angry with me and that was the cause of things happening to me. So, I became angry with myself for causing trouble for myself. I realized that anger was an issue and asked the Lord to help me. I recommitted my life to Christ after causing Him shame and trouble for myself. I started to tell Him how I felt, and He began to tell me what I needed to do. I started spending time and fellowship with Him and that was when I started to deal with anger. I was afraid to abuse my children because of my past and asked the Lord to help me.

He allowed me to raise my children to know Him and fear Him. They were baptized as teenagers and continue in the faith. The Lord has given me a wonderful daughter-in-law and two grandchildren. The Lord had done a work through me and had helped to address conflicts and deal with my temper. I have chosen to use wisdom in dealing with daily issues instead of displaying anger. The Lord has taught me how to live in peace and share peace with others. I take all my concerns to the Lord and wait for Him to tell me what to do. I depend on God for everything because I know He cares.

How Conflicts Affect Living

Living is hard when people live with unresolved conflicts. Unresolved conflicts can create anger, frustration and depression. Resolving conflict can be difficult, but the scriptures offers us help in this area. Proverbs 15:18 tells us that hot temper produces arguments, but patience creates peace. The word teaches us to love those who hate and persecutes us. Also, we should speak well of others. In Romans 12:17-18, Paul tells us to live peaceable with everyone if all possible. There is a blessing for the peace maker. Some conflicts can be resolved by making peace.

Forgiveness is another way to resolve conflicts. This shows we love, and care for the person we are forgiving. Taking revenge and showing hatred cannot resolve conflicts. This will prolong conflict and set the stage for bitterness and anger (Ephesians 4:31-32). If you brother sins, go to him in private and show him his faults. If he listens to you, you have won him, and the conflict is resolved. If he refuses to listen, take one or two witness and confirmed the facts with them. If he continues to refuse after all this, then take him to the church body for its intervention. Finally, if he continues to refuse, leave him alone because you have done all you can to resolve the conflict.

Words are powerful and can be damaging depending on how we use them. Harsh words or speech cannot resolve conflicts. A harsh word is like a sword thrust at an individual (Proverbs 12:18). Wisdom helps in word choice because this helps with word selection. Kind words bring healing. They reduce tension and resolve conflict. Paul believes that words spoken in love are righteous and brings joy and happiness to people. James cautioned us to be quick to hear but slow to speak because it is important that we examine our words so as not to create anger (James 1:19-20).

Paul also cautioned against unwholesome words, as they do not bring edification but rather harm and distress. Conflict will be resolved if our words bring grace and edification to the hearer. We can live in harmony when we use kind and sympathetic words instead of insulting words. A gentle answer turns away wrath, but harsh words stir up anger (Proverbs 15:1). Living is easy when we respect every man and leave vengeance to God because it belongs to Him.

Rebellion

Living is hard when we become stubborn, reject the word of God, and develop the spirit of independence. Samuel compares rebellion to witchcraft, iniquity and idolatry (1 Samuel 15:23). Rejection of the word of God is like rejecting His favor over our lives. This evil has prevented the rebellious person from hearing from God because the nature of God is unable to tolerate sin. Sin is a separation from God. According to Proverbs 17:11, a rebellious man is an evil man. Living is difficult because the rebellious dwells in a dry land (Psalm 68:6).

The rebellious will serve his enemies, be hungry and naked. He does not love the Lord and is unable to keep the commandment. The devil is the father of the rebellious. Living is hard when we are drawn away by our own evil desires. Evil desires will give birth to sin. Sin, when fully grown, will give birth to death (James 1:14). Rebellion leads to filthy conduct and wickedness. We were created with the void to depend on the creator. The spirit of independence will lead to rebellion. We cannot live and do what we want or as we please. In Him we live, move and breathe (Acts 17:28). We were bought with a price, the blood of Jesus.

Living is easy when we understand that every good gift come from Jesus. Until we start living in the will of Christ, that is when we will receive the blessings. We will then escape the corruption of the world. In the scriptures, rebellion is made like the sin of divination and the rejection of the Word of God (1 Samuel 15:23). According to Proverbs 17:11, an evil man seeks rebellion.

Experience

It is the nature of human beings to manipulate and do things their way. It is easy to want to manipulate because of the pressures, burdens, heartache and trouble. Like Jacob, we want to wrestle with what we believe. As children, we try to manipulate our parents, try to control the narrative and take control. So, we rebel to change things around us, get what we desire instead of doing what God wants us to do. We do not have to rebel; when there is pressure in our lives, all we must do is to call on God. He loves us and will get us through.

How To Deal With Trials And Temptations

The scriptures teach us to rejoice in trials, whether we like them or not, they are going to come. We are encouraged to count it all but joy when we meet trials (James 1:2). Living is difficult when we are saddened by trials and unable to overcome them. Some people will have a pity party and invite people to mourn and grieve with them indefinitely. Some even go to the extreme and blame others.

Many of the trials and temptation we face and degree of hardship cannot be remedied by us. They were not meant for us to solve but meant to teach us patience and strengthen us. We need the spirit of God to help us when we go through these situations. The minute we realize this and become joyful in the situation, then we will see a way out because we now minimize the situation and maximize the Lord. In the event of trouble, the human mind wants to mourn and grieve as oppose to rejoice.

People normally become sad, talk about the situation to friends before praying and hoping for change. We are told to be patient, prayerful and rejoice in hope (Romans 12:12). Tribulations come to strengthen us as believers. They come to encourage us to continue because we know we cannot enter the kingdom of God without tribulations (Acts 14:22). Nothing can separate us from the love of God. Our lives are precious to the Lord. He has redeemed us unto Himself and loved us with an everlasting love.

Many do not understand the value of trials and temptation. People sometimes think that when they accept Christ that trials will end. On the other hand, it would appear to be the beginning of trouble. Living is easy when we obey the Word of God because he brings out families bound with chains, but the rebellious remains in dry land (Psalm 68:6). There are some people who do not pray and think about the goodness of God until they have trouble.

Therefore, trials and temptation are good for many people because that keeps them in line. On the other hand, living is hard when people put themselves in trouble. According to James 4:17, the person who knows what is good and decides to do otherwise is guilty of sin. So, there are people who knowingly do wrong things because it either pleases them or satisfies their selfish ambitions. Living is hard for those people.

Chapter 10
Courage

Courage may be defined as the ability to do something extraordinary, something you never thought you could have accomplished or faced. Living is hard when we lose courage and become discouraged. The strength, bravery or valor to confront a problem or situation is what God expects of us. We are expected to resist the opposition of our enemies and remain firm even when we face danger or difficulty. Courage is one of the qualities of the spirit. It is a choice that we make to do the will of Christ without intimidation or fear. Courage will come when we put our trust in God.

He told us that tough challenges will come, but they will not overtake us or destroy us because He will never leave us or forsake us. Living is easy when we demonstrate courage. The sense of acting appropriately in a difficult situation is controlled by the Holy Spirit. Doing so will help us to achieve the good things of life, overcome the things that are threatening and develop humility in Christ. Intimidation and fear are tools used by the enemy discourage us, but firmness in mind in the spirit helps us to develop boldness.

As children of Christ, we are called to be bold because we are fighting from a position of victory. This is a moral courage that we should display daily so that the world will know who we represent. Courageous believers are strong in their knowledge of Christ and recognize who they are in Christ. They are confident that they can do all things through Christ who gives strength (Philippians 4:13).

Living is easy when we become passionate and live with purpose. Therefore, we need to recognize the importance of Christ in our lives and having Him lead us daily. He gives us the boldness, and the assurance that with Him all things are possible. Whatever our circumstances are, He will give us the strength to handle them is a way that pleases Him. In Hebrews 10:35-36, Paul reminded us not to lose courage because it comes with a great reward; a high price was paid by the Lord for us. We need to exercise patience when doing the will of God so that we can receive His promises.

Life is about survival, going through the circumstances and situations present but, overcoming them. We are losing the fight anytime we take it up in our own hands. We need to stand boldly and declare who God is, the same way David declare who his God was. God did not call quitters; He has called us to be strong and tough so that we can handle the challenges of the time. In all my life I have never seen a quitter win but courage always wins. That is what we are called to be courageous: that is how we win.

How To Identify The Enemy: Strategy To Win

Living is hard when we think flesh and blood are our enemy. Ephesians 6:12 tells us that the struggle is not against flesh and blood but against principalities and powers, the rulers of darkness in this world, spiritual wickedness in high places. Life is easy when we put on the whole armor of God that we may be able to stand against the schemes of the enemy. When we direct our energy to fight others, it shows that we have no understanding of the magnitude of the fight or what we are fighting.

We must understand that our God is a consuming fire. In the book of Kings (2 Kings 19:14-35), Hezekiah received threat of destruction by the kings of Assyria. He went to the temple, and there told his God about the threats. We must know who we are and who is fighting for us. Our father God promised to defend us against the enemy. That night, the angel of the Lord destroyed 185,000 Assyrians. Hezekiah did not even respond to the enemy's threat. So, the next time we are threatened by the enemy, instead of addressing the enemy, we should go the Lord and let Him fight for us. We can be assured that our enemies will be defeated.

He is the helper of the helpless and the defender of the weak. It does not matter the number of the enemy. Our God can never lose a fight. He is a mighty warrior, great in battle, Jehovah is His name. When the enemy takes us to his court of accusation, we should then consult with the high court of Heaven against them. The intended evil against us cannot be performed (Psalm 21:11). The Lord will turn them back by sending arrows against them when we praise the Lord. Jesus is the friend who adheres closer than a brother.

We know from the word that all things work together for good to those who love the Lord (Romans 8:28). These are whom He has called to His purpose. If God be for us, then who can come against us? According to Romans 8:25, none can separate from the love of Christ. Living is difficult when we are unable to identify our enemies. Some of our prominent enemies are fear, doubt, discouragement, weariness, fatigue, distraction and self. The enemies we perceive as giants are mere grasshoppers in the sight of God. Gideon was able to identify the cowards, those who faint easily and separate them from the courageous, the strong and the brave.

Victory requires the ability to identify, discern and know those who are against you. The real enemy is the devil. Unfortunately, he uses people as agents and forces against us. We cannot allow our circumstances to shake us. We need to stand firm on the solid rock that is Jesus Christ. He promised not to leave us or forsake us.

Prayer As A Weapon Of Choice

Prayer is an important ingredient for easy living. Our prayer life will help to shape and dictate the outcome of the events in our lives. On the other hand, a weak prayer life will make living hard and unpredictable. In Colossians 1:3-12, Paul exalted the brethren on the importance of prayer and how prayer impacts our daily lives. We are reminded to always give thanks to God the father of our faith. This faith points us to the hope stored up in heaven.

Praying to God will help us to strengthen our faith, bear fruit and grow. By so doing, we can understand God's grace in a way to make it applicable to our lives. Prayer helps us to understand faithfulness and love and appreciate others. A constant interaction with the Holy Spirit fills us with wisdom, knowledge and understanding how to live and please God in every way. As we pray and seek God, He allows us to grow and be strengthened in His power.

The strength of the Lord helps us to develop patience and endurance, which we need to live a successful and productive life. This will help us to be joyful, add value and quality to our lives as we share the inheritance, He has for us. Living is easy when we understand how to fellowship and give intimate worship and prayer to the Lord. We are encouraged to pray without ceasing. Jesus told us in Matthew 18 that if any two should agree on earth concerning anything our heavenly father will grant it. When we pray in the name of Jesus, He gives us power and authority in the Holy Spirit.

He promises to deliver us from darkness into His marvelous light as the beloved of Christ. Prayer is one way to getting connected as a beloved child. Only He can forgive and grant us redemption. Prayer helps us to achieve this gift. Living will be easy as we continue to live the promise of victory when we pray. The earlier we realize that when we pray and seek God, it is then we understand the characteristic of grace. This knowledge and understanding helps us to live holy and faithful.

Courage

Peace in God will be achieved as we give love and respect to God in prayer and thanksgiving. Faith and love yields hope in the equation.

God has already done His part; all that is left for us to do in life is to do our part by trusting in His saving grace. Hope is stored up for us, and grace and peace come from our father in heaven. Prayer helps us to understand truth and the gospel of Jesus Christ. The truth of the Gospel is what helps us to live transformed lives. This gives us the capacity to prosper and bear fruits even in times of adversity or trouble.

Living is easy because we can do none of this by ourselves, we must rely on Jesus. Prayer will help us to develop the spirit of joy and thanksgiving. Diligent prayer helps us to be alert because we open our eyes and heart to Jesus. One of the benefits of prayer is contentment in His words as we choose to live life from God's prospective. Prayer helps us to repent; God's forgiveness will come with grace and mercy.

The Lord Jesus is the only one who can rest our hearts and minds when there are trials and temptations. Praying to the Lord will allow us to be mentally and physically prepared to face challenges in life. James encourages us to think of testing and trials as pure joy as they come to make us stronger. Jesus has overcome the world, and this makes us overcomers as well. As we continue to pray and seek the Lord, we are reminded of His goodness because all things work together for good to those who love the Lord. God's love and unforgiveness is limitless to us. Frustration and tiredness are meant to discourage us, but for the Lord, they are meant to strengthen us.

The Lord wants us to be strong and persistent. A prayer of perseverance will encourage us to seek the Lord diligently for guidance. The Lord has promised us wisdom and guidance if we trust in Him. As we continue to pray and trust God, He grants us healing, deliverance and power. Prayer will help you to live the way God wants you to live and that is easy. A weak or inconsistent prayer life will make living difficult. In Colossians 1:3-12, Paul stressed the importance of prayer.

Our faith is strengthened when we pray to the Lord. Increased faith levels promote growth and help us to bear fruit. An understanding the grace of God and applying grace to our lives makes living easier. The scripture encourages us to be faithful even in our payer life. Faithfulness is learnt through consistent prayer. We can also learn to love each other in consistent interaction with the Holy Spirit. The Holy Spirit will fill us with knowledge, wisdom and understanding. This will help us to love and please the Lord.

Living is easy when our lives please the Lord. Strength from the Lord will boost our endurance and teach us patience. Patience will help us to see the hand of God in our lives. We will receive our inheritance when we fellowship with the Lord in worship and prayer. Paul encourages us to pray for one another constantly. Doing so, will cause an agreement. Jesus told us that if any two agree on earth concerning any matter, our heavenly father shall grant it.

Jesus gives us power and authority when we pray in His name. The Holy Spirit then fills us with the knowledge of God's will for our lives. He then enlightens us with spiritual wisdom and understanding. This makes living easy as we continue to trust the process. Prayer helps us to live in accordance with the word of God. The Lord will deliver us from darkness and transfer us into His kingdom as the beloved. Jesus is the only one who can grant us redemption and forgive our sins. Therefore, living will become easy for us because He had already given us victory before we pray. We will become holy and faithful as we continue to pray, seek God and understand the characteristic of grace.

Testimony

My personal experiences with the Lord tell me that there is nothing the Lord cannot do. These experiences have made me to think the way God thinks. I know that the way man thinks is demonic and not of God. So, when situation arises, I call on God, get into the word and agree with what God says about the situation. Whatever is happening in my life or whatever the challenges, I see victory. Victory is sure even though I do not know when it is coming. My friend told me of a couple who wanted to be in fulltime ministry and were facing financial challenges. They both agree that the wife would work while the husband do ministry full time.

So, they prayed for a job close to home, transportation, benefit and a desired salary. At the time they prayed, they did not have a place in mind. Even though they did not know where to apply, they trusted their God. Two months after they prayed a new company came into town. They heard of the new company and the wife applied for a position. To their surprise, they called her in for an interview. They offered the salary she desired, the same amount she prayed for, the position came with a car and the job was located at exactly the distance she had asked. They knew that God would provide, especially when we want to do His will. He is the one who gives hope and victory. God's word cannot be reversed: whatever He says is forever settled.

Repentance To Gain Recognition In The Kingdom

Repentance is central in Christianity. Jesus told us in Matthew 4:17 to repent because the kingdom of God is coming. Living is hard when we live in sin because the kingdom of God cannot come to us. If the kingdom of God cannot come to us, then God cannot dwell in our lives. The kingdom of God can only come to those who recognize their sins and confess them to God. God is merciful and will forgive us when we repent. Living is hard when we continue to sin and refuse to repent. The kingdom of God is righteousness, peace and joy in the Holy Ghost.

God is the one who grants repentance. True faith will make us new and free. A genuine repentance is a negative relation toward sin and a positive attitude toward righteousness. Living is hard when we try to hide sin. We are expected to confess sin, give them up and turn away to righteousness. It is then that we will be able to walk by the prompting of the Holy Spirit. The Holy Spirit brings quietness, rest and peace. Turning from sin is a purification experience that brings deliverance, power, wholeness and spiritual preservation. Happiness and joy are experienced after repentance.

Living is hard when we try to conceal our sins. Those who conceal their sins will not prosper. We must confess and denounce our sins to find mercy and forgiveness (Proverbs 28:13). Living is easy when we repent because the Lord promises to refresh us. He is gracious and compassionate to those who repent. Repentance brings healing, both physical and spiritual. This leads us to the knowledge and truth of Christ. We are placed into a position of understanding of His love and mercy.

Living is hard when we refuse to repent because we create a separation between us and God. The hand of God is blocked by unrepented sin. Those who refuse to repent are referred to as wicked (Ezekiel 18:21-23). There are many rewards associated with repentance. We escape the curse when we repent. Also, the Lord will bring us back to Himself from where we were scattered, made captives and lost our possession. He promised restoration to those who repent, punished their enemies, and make them fruitful (Deuteronomy 30:1-10).

Forgiveness To Access Mercy

We have heard it said many times unforgiveness is like drinking poison and expecting someone with whom you have differences to die. Holding grudges seems to only affect the one who holds them and not necessarily those held against. Forgiveness is an act of pardon or mercy. The scriptures have much to say about forgiveness. Jesus taught us about forgiveness and emphasized a condition for it.

We can see it clearly in the Lord's prayer. If we do not forgive each other's wrongdoing, our heavenly father will not forgive us of our wrongdoing (Matthew 6:14). When we forgive others, our heavenly father will forgive us. We should get rid of all bitterness, passion and anger. Being kind and tenderhearted to each other will help us to live a less stressful life.

Living is hard when we harbor bitterness against each other. Living is easy when we forgive because we are guaranteed mercy. Grace is available to us when we follow the instruction of Christ. If we confess our sins to God, He will forgive us of our sins and purify us from all our wrongdoing (1 John 1:9). Spiritual strength will come to those who are forgiven and bring an ease to living. Bitterness and anger will produce a life of hardship, hunger and nakedness. Therefore, unforgiveness will bring sickness and disease.

Victory requires the ability to identify, discern and know those who are against you. The real enemy is the devil. Unfortunately, he uses people as agents and forces against us. We cannot allow our circumstances to shake us. We need to stand firm on the solid rock which is Jesus Christ. He promised not to leave us or forsake us shake us.

Testimony

There was a man in my district that was very bitter against his neighbor. This man has not spoken to his neighbor for ten years. His became sick and all ten fingers were disfigured. He could no longer take care of himself and asked other neighbors for help. He continues to say unkind things about the neighbor who did him wrong and continued to be bitter. One of the neighbors who came to help him prayed for him and told him to forgive that neighbor but he refused. This neighbor continues to pray for him and talk to him. As he continued to pray for him and talk to the Lord about this man, the Lord told him the crippled man has not forgiven ten people and that was the reason for his disability. The disfigured man prayed the sinner's prayer. He started to attend church. A pastor out of town visited his church, and he preached about forgiveness. An altar call was made, and he responded to the call. Nine of his ten fingers were healed, they were no longer crippled except one finger. The man went home with one crippled finger and could not understand why he was not completely healed. The same neighbor who led him to Christ visited. He too could not understand why one finger was still crippled and thought it is left for a reminder. The man with the crippled finger refused to be satisfied.

The next week he went to church and everyone was amazed when they saw what had happened. The man with the crippled finger was not completely satisfied and refused to believe that that finger remained as a reminder. The pastor asked him to explain what he had done prior to receiving healing to the nine fingers. He said he had forgiven everyone except his neighbor because he is a wicked man. The pastor begged him to release the neighbor as that could be the reason for the incomplete healing. The man agreed to work on his forgiveness. A week later the other finger started to show signs of change, and eventually, it was healed. This man started going around telling and showing how God healed him and encourages others to forgive.

Chapter 11

RELATIONSHIP AND SHAPING LIVES

Relationship is a need for everyone while we are here on earth. It is imperative that we understand relationships and the role different relationship plays in our life. A key element in a relationship is to help us understand the nature of a relationship. In addition, we need to understand the reason for the relationship. That is, when the relationship begins, when it ends, and the characteristics of the relationship.

God is the author of our lives, but He has given the freedom to determine who enters and leaves our lives. So, before we get into relationships, we should ask the Lord if these relationships are right for us. He will determine if the relationship will be beneficial or not. People join relationships for different reasons: benefits, financial gains, emotional gains, security, status and ideology.

Whatever the relationship is about, we are in control of these relationships and may terminate them at any time. Wisdom is a principal thing for any relationship to be successful. We need to recognize the characteristics of the individual in the relationship and the intent for wanting to be in a relationship. If the intent is to gain selfish ambition or a financial goal, then the relationship may one that will be short lived. So, prior to starting any relationship, this should be made clear on day one in order to minimize conflicts and emotional distress.

Living is hard when we surround ourselves with doubters and negative individuals. We need to surround ourselves with positive and courageous people. In life, everyone around you is not for you and with you. Some people are not with you because they are jealous of you or people will see their weakness. Surround yourself with people of faith, people who believe and trust God. According to Proverbs 13: 20, he who walks with wise men will be wise, but he who walks with fools will be destroyed. People are jealous of your dreams and success, and they are afraid to lose your friendship.

Therefore, it is pertinent that you evaluate the motives of those who come into your life. There are also those who come into your life to take from your life and absorb your time. These persons are drainers, their conversation is meant to distract, decrease, and devalue your life. This parasitic effect is meant to diminish you and to eventually destroy you. Living is a challenge with these relationships, and it is only wise to terminate these relationships. The earlier we can detect the negative energy and address it, the better the outcome. Wisdom teaches us to surround ourselves with people who are wise, and Christ is their foundation.

God in His infinite mercy and grace will help us to identify these individuals and exclude them from our lives, which will make us productive and prosperous. Christ has come to rescue us and give us life. We must know when to let people go. We cannot control what people do, but we can keep people out of our lives. Everyone who comes into our lives are not all well-wishers; they are assigned by the enemy to create havoc in our lives.

If they are not there to lift you up, they come to pull you down. If they are not an addition, then they are a subtraction. If they are not there as an encourager, they will be a discourager. They all have a motive, and we need to know what that motive is. We need to separate ourselves from double-minded people. James 1 tells us a double-minded man is unstable and cannot receive anything form the Lord. When we surround ourselves with people of faith who do not waver, we will receive from God. There is power in agreement.

Many people come into your life just to criticize you. You can do nothing right for them. They think they own you and can dictate what you do and how you live your life. We do not have to acknowledge and respond to the critics, but we can let them know, for sure, that the Lord is the master of our lives. He will never fail us or disappoint us. He is a gracious and loving God, and He is all that we need.

Life is easy when we recognized and accepted those who are sent by God and opposed those sent by the enemy. We must let go of the dividers, the blockers, those who limit and manipulates. Also, the doubters, the negative, the dream killers and the dream stealers. God has given us choices and wisdom to make decisions for our lives. Therefore, we have the ability hire and fire people from our lives. We need to understand seasonal relationships and learn to let people go when their season expires. If we allow some people can stay in our lives, they will bring heartache and disappointment.

It is only when these people leave your life that drama and strife ends. Not everyone who comes into our life brings success. We must know what to receive and what to reject for our life. That means we must reject the lies of the enemy because Satan comes to steal kill and destroy (John 10:10).

Jesus instructs us to love one another and welcome strangers because we could be entertaining angels (Hebrew 13: 1-2). The scriptures also teach us to obey our leaders and follow their orders. Our leaders have the responsibility to watch over our souls. The leaders will give account of their service to the Lord. Being obedient to our leaders will make their work easier and bring them joy in doing their work (Hebrews 13:17).

Relationship With Christ And Living

Our relationship with Christ will determine the kind of life we live. If we put Christ first and trust in the Lord, we will be successful in all endeavors. The Lord told Joshua to be strong and courageous and to focus on Him. He also assured us that we will prosper in the way of the Lord. If we meditate on the words of the Lord day and night, the Lord will make us prosperous and will direct us in all his ways (Joshua 1:1-10).

Unless we live our lives this way, our lives will be meaningless, and living will be hard. The Lord promised to be with us wherever we go and protect us. We can depend on Jesus to take care of us. His promises are forever settled in heaven. The closer we walk with Jesus, the more we become strong in Him. As we walk with Him, the challenges in life will become minute because Jesus will be magnified in our lives. Consequently, life will be easy for us. Victory is only possible in Jesus. He wears the victor's crown, making us victorious with him. God is fighting for us; therefore, we cannot be defeated. We are called to live a life above reproach.

According to Titus 3:2, we should not speak evil of anyone but be gentle showing meekness unto all men. Living will be hard if we become disobedient and lend our self to hatred, bitterness, malice and envy. We should live blameless and good steward of the Lord (Titus 1: 6-9) and faithful to him. Our labor will not be in vain if we labor for the Lord. Life is easy when we offer sacrifice and service to the Lord. We must live everyday with the mind of Christ. We should live as children of God. Psalm 1 tells us that blessed is the man who does not walk in the counsel of the ungodly or stands in the way of sinners.

His delight is in the law of the Lord, and in it, he meditates day and night. He will be like a tree that brings forth good fruit at the appointed time or season. The Lord dwells with His people; they are safe, and no evil can come near the dwelling of the Lord. Life is easy in the dwelling of the Lord. The Lord said he will never leave us or forsake us. He will show up strong and powerful when we are in dire situations and condemnation. He showed up for Daniel when he was thrown in the lion's den, the three Hebrew boys when they were thrown in the lake of fire.

God never fails to defend His children. All we need to do is to acknowledge our faults and repent of our sins. Psalm 38:16 tells us that

Relationship And Shaping Lives

He will be there when our foot slip and when we declare our iniquity and become sorry for our sins. Jeremiah told us that He has great plans for us; He knows our destiny. We can be all that God wants us to be if we let go of condemnation and hold onto Jesus. God can do greater than we can ever ask, think or imagine. We should be intimate in our faith and guard ourselves from strange teachings. This will help us to increase our inner strength in Christ.

Living is hard when we lack the zeal or desire to go after our desires and aspirations. People often say they are trying very hard to accomplish their vision, but the degree of persistence is difficult to measure. Desperate people take desperate measures; these people are usually the achievers. Great athletes will tell you that they will train for several hours to prepare themselves for a single race. The word tells us that those who hunger and thirst for righteousness sake shall be filled.

Jesus told His disciples that some problems can only be solves with prayer and fasting. We may need to make sacrifices in our lives to achieve the things we desire. This may require us to address the physiologic, emotional or physical needs. . When we come into the presence of the Lord, our priority is to worship. Our zeal for God comes with unity. Sacrificing ourselves for the work of the Lord requires us to die to sin daily. The Lord requires us to work diligently for Him. We cannot receive the blessing when we walk outside the will of God. It is the will of the Lord for us to live in unity concerning his work.

God has given us the authority to destroy anything that gets into the way of our worship. Where there is a lack of zeal, there is no unity. Doubt and division will creep in when there is no zeal for the things of the Lord. The enemy will come in and create havoc in our lives where zeal and unity are absent. In 1 Corinthians 15:31, Paul boasted that his zeal for Christ required him to die daily to fulfill the work of Christ.

Jesus gives us power and authority when we pray in His name. The Holy Spirit then fills us with the knowledge of Gods will for our lives. He then enlightens us with spiritual wisdom and understanding. This makes living easy as we continue to trust the process. Prayer helps us to live in accordance with the word of God. The Lord will deliver us from darkness and transfer us into His kingdom as the beloved. Jesus is the only one who can grant us redemption and forgive our sins. Therefore, living will become easy for us because He had already given us victory before we pray. We will become holy and faithful as we continue to pray, seek God and understand the characteristic of grace.

Idolatory And Its Effect On Living

Living is hard when we embrace idolatry in our lives. If we embrace idolatry, the spirit of the Lord is unable to operate in our lives. Many people say they know the Lord, but there is nothing in their lives that suggest that the Lord is working in their lives. Their focus is really on the gods of the earth. Many have built alters in their lives and place men, material and possessions before God.

The scriptures tell us that we should not have any other God before Him. The gods of this world are idols; they are useless and helpless. The Lord God has made heaven and earth (Psalm 96:5). Some people desire things from the Lord, but they have other gods ruling their lives. These people are not in position to receive from God. Isaiah 44:6-48 speaks of the foolishness of idols.

The Lord of heaven stated that He is the first and the last; there is no other God but Him. The idols that people worship is useless and cannot help them. All these idols are doing is ruining their lives because they are blind, deaf and mute. These idols are hindering them in many ways. They cannot hear God when He speaks, feel His presence or see His glory. Idol worshipers have set themselves up for failure and destruction. The objects of worship are worthless, shameful and disgraceful and unacceptable to the God of heaven. He is unable to relate to the idol worshipers except to punish them.

Idol worshipers are not able to know God because they have too many gods. They are unable to distinguish between who or what can help. They become confused, and they lack knowledge and understanding.

Relationship And Shaping Lives

According to Matthew 6:24, no man can serve two masters. He will love one and despise the other. Those who serve foreign gods are unable to acknowledge the true and living God. The spirit of God is unable to work in the double minded and the idol worshipers. The idol worshiper is spiritually cut off from God. The idol worshiper is unable to commune with God, sing hymns and spiritual songs because their heart is far from God. Living is hard for the idol worshipers.

They are ruled by the god of this world and are separated from God. A life of idolatry is one of sin and an invitation of the wrath of God. In Exodus 43:14, He tells us not to worship any other God because He is a jealous God. Living is easy when we recognize that Jesus is Lord and give Him all the glory and the praise. He promises never to leave us or forsake us. As we continue to walk in the ways of the Lord, He promises to bless us. We will receive a blessing from the Lord. We will not have to worry about food, clothing and shelter.

He is our provider and protector. Acts 3:19 tells us that when we repent of our sins, they will be blotted out, and the times of refreshing shall come from the presence of the Lord. Living is easy when the Lord refreshes our lives. A refreshed life is full of strength, love and happiness. We are now considered the righteousness of Christ as He dwells in us.

Testimony

A friend called me a while back very frantic to let me know that she had lost her husband. I remembered it was an incredibly sad day. We sought the Lord and asked for peace and how to proceed. I sat down and as I listened to what she was saying and how she was talking about how great a person he was. She said she did not know to move forward in the coming weeks and months because he was doing everything. She said many things, but there was one thing that stood out to me. She mentioned it was her fault because she made him her idol. Her exact words were "I worshiped my husband. That is why God took him from me".

God does not want us to put anything or anyone before Him. I have seen people who worship their children, home, car, job and even other people. Sometimes we need to evaluate our lives and, ask ourselves if there is anyone or anything that is taking the place of Christ. Anything or anyone we put before God is an idol that displeases God. There are things we may ask God for, and He may not grant us because He knows when we get it, our focus will change and our relationship will change with Him. God will work everything for our good.

Chapter 12

How Wealth Affects Living

The word of God tells us that if riches increase, not to set our mind on it. Living is hard if you depend on earthly things and material possession. In Luke 42:16, the rich man trusted in his abundance. Riches can take wings and fly away. Life is easy when we put our trust in the Lord. He is our source, provider and defender. Earthly things are temporary and bring disappointment when we put our trust in them. In Timothy 6:15, Paul told Timothy to instruct the rich to trust in God, not in uncertain riches.

Those of us who are rich should ask the Lord to guide us from placing faith in the wrong place. Matthew 6: 19-20 tells us not to lay up for ourselves treasures on earth because they can be destroyed by moth or rust or stolen by thieves. Living is hard when you live to store up treasures on earth. Life is easy when you store up treasures in heaven where thieves cannot break in and moth and rust cannot destroy. Those who make material things their source of peace and joy will soon discover the opposite as living becomes hard.

The Lord is the peace giver; those whose minds are set on worldly pleasure would have shut out Christ out of their lives. Living will become even harder as the wrath of God visits the disobedient and ungodly. Loss of worldly treasures will result in physical and emotional distress. We can avoid devastation and despair if we live according to the word of God. Life is easy when we realize that Christ is our life and, when He appears, we shall appear with Him (Colossians 3:4).

Authority

Authority comes from God. It is instituted by God, and we His people are subjected to governing authorities. If we reject God's authority, we reject His institution and resist His appointed. We get God's approval when we please Him. We can please Him by obeying His authority (Romans 13:1-7). Living is hard when people live in fear of authority. Doing what is right according to the will of God will force authority to respect and honor people. According to Romans 13:13, we are expected to submit to governing authority because they are put in place by God.

Therefore, when we rebel against authority, it is considered rebellion against the Lord. Punishment is promised to those who rebel against God. Authority is meant to punish those who rebel and reward those who obey. Compliance with authority is a principle we should all adapt and should not cause us to fear. Living is easy when we live without fear of punishment and with a clear conscience. So then, we should honor those in authority.

As we try to honor Godly principles on earth, we can all live in love and enjoy happy and prosperous lives. That is, we would not wrong our neighbors and help to win the unsaved to Christ. In obedience to the word of God, we cannot participate in darkness and immoral living. Living is easy when we do not indulge in immoral desires. God has given us spiritual powers over the enemy. Submission to the will of God gives us power to resist the enemy. God is the one who gives us the authority to bind and loose on earth (Matthew 18:18-20). The Lord will do what we ask if we come into the agreement with Him.

Living is easy when we live our lives in agreement with the Lord. God is the keeper of our soul. He has given us the power to destroy

How Wealth Affects Living

strongholds in our lives. The Lord will allow us to experience signs and wonders when we submit our lives to Him. As we continue to believe in the Lord and His powers, He gives us the power to cast out demons, speak in new tongues, lay hands on the sick and see them recover, Also we are promised that we will not be hurt from poison, by contact or ingested.

According to Mark 16:17-18, no one can submit to the Lord unless he is born of God. Those who are born of Christ are overcomers of the world. That means, we have victory over the world through our faith in Christ Jesus. When we submit to Christ, He gives us the spirit of truth. The spirit of truth is what guides us in all truth. Living is easy when we are guided by the spirit of truth. The spirit of truth will guide us to live holy lives. We will be led to present our bodies as a living sacrifice to the Lord. Our minds will be transformed, and the will of God will be made plain to us.

Living is easy when we engage in the acceptable and perfect will of God for our lives (Romans 12:1-21). The Lord will make us to be sober and provide us with the appropriate measure of faith to function in our daily lives. The Lord's intention from the beginning was that man should have dominion over the earth and all living things on the earth. Living is easy when we live the reality and the authority that God has given unto us.

The Lord has promised to defeat our enemies and have dominion over them. Our God has all authority, and He has given us the kingdom, the power and the glory. He is the ruler of the world and gives authority to whomever He pleases (Daniel 4:17). The sooner we realize the authority that is given unto us and understand the magnitude of the power He has given unto us, the more determined we will be to live as overcomers. Jesus himself has overcome the world and has given us the same power to overcome.

Authority is a gift of freedom. Freedom will provide us with joy, peace and happiness. Living is easy when we realize that the plans God has for us are plans to prosper us and not to harm us. They are plans to give us hope and a future (Jerimiah 29:11). Living is easy as we continue to trust in Him and live according to His plans for us.

How Choices Affect Living

Living is easy when we make correct choices in life and is difficult when we make silly and selfish choices. God has given us free will and freedom too chose. He knew before we were created the choices we would make and made provision for us to redeem us. Even though these plans were put in place for us, we would not know them if we did not read the scriptures to learn of them. One thing for sure, abiding by the standards God has for us will keep us safe, and living will become easy. According to Proverbs 22, if we are given the choice between good reputation and great wealth, we should choose good reputation over wealth.

Wealth can afford can material things and relationships with people, but it cannot buy good reputation. Good reputation comes from the Lord. He makes it affordable for both the rich and the poor. Being able to make sensible choices in life will help us to see trouble and avoid them. Those who make bad choices will walk into trouble and regret them later. Living is hard when we make bad choices because they lead to unwanted consequences

Therefore, it is in our best interest to make good choices and guard ourselves from repulsiveness. We can guard our lives by obeying the Lord. The word of God has taught us to be humble and trust the Lord. This will bring us wealth, honor and long life. That is, we should choose good reputation. Good reputation only comes from the Lord. Living is easy when we love our lives. Loving our lives is shown when we live holy and reputable lives. We will not be caught by the traps set for the wicked. We are taught in the scriptures that those who borrow money are slaves to the lender. God's plan for those he has called and loved is not to be slaves to the rich. He wants us to be lenders and not borrowers, above and not beneath (Deuteronomy 28:12-13).

Living is hard when we make excuses and admit seeds of injustice to come into our lives by the people we allow into our lives. Sometimes, we allow conceited people, proud people and contentious people. These are usually those who have rejected the will of God and will bring destruction into our lives. We also allow lazy and doubtful people into our homes, our business, lives and relationships. Allowing those who indulge in sin into our lives will bring destruction and shame to our lives. Sin and ungodliness will destroy us.

Living is easy when we choose people who are pure and kind and love the Lord to be part of our lives. The Lord promises to bless us when we are generous and share with the poor. Those who help the poor lends to the Lord (Proverbs 19:17). Those who are self-righteous and reject God, and His love should not be allowed to be part of our lives. The reason is that their intension would be to corrupt the relationship and make living difficult.

How Covenants And Pledges Affect Living

A covenant is an agreement between God and man. God is the one who makes the agreement and gives the condition. The agreement comes to man with the promise to bless man if he obeys. People also makes earthly agreements, and God expects us to honor these agreements. God expects us to keep our vows and act on them without delay (Ecclesiastes 5:4).

Living is hard when we do not keep the covenants of the Lord. According to Deuteronomy 29:9, the Lord reminded us that if we keep the words His covenant, we would prosper in all that we do. We can only be established by the Lord when we keep the oath entered in with the Lord. In our lifetime, we have made several pledges to the Lord and promised Him to be faithful if He delivered us. Some we have kept, and others we have not. Some we remembered and others we forget. Many of the hardship we face could have been the result of unkept promises and the Lord is reminding us to revisit those promises. Even if forget these promises, God is not man and cannot forget.

Many of the promises we make, covenants we come under are associated with curses when they were not honored. The covenant may have been associated with our family, heath, finances, ministry or calling. An unkept covenant is an act of disobedience; this is evidence that the heart has turned from God. A heart that has turned from God cannot experience joy and peace. That is, this heart is unable to accept and acknowledge grace. Therefore, we need to repent of our disobedience to the Lord and ask for forgiveness to make living easy. It is important that we remember covenants and repent of unkept ones to prevent curses.

Conclusion

Life is a gift. The scriptures tell us that Jesus laid down His life for us freely. He died so that we may live. We should be grateful for every day we see and show our gratitude to the Lord. He is our creator, and He has given to us all the resources we need to be successful in life. This is what makes living easy because when we put our trust in the Lord, He takes care of us. He protects and provides for us. We can rest assured that He will be there for us. Living is easy when we trust the Lord. He is the way, the truth and the life.

Although life comes with its challenges, twists and turns, patterning the principles set by the Lord guarantees success. He strengthens the weak and encourages the brokenhearted. The Lord wants us to wait on Him so that our strength will be renewed in times of adversity. When we wait on the Lord, the Holy Spirit directs our lives and becomes our counselor. The Lord will come with strong hands when we call Him and carry us in His bosom to safety (Isaiah 40:11). Living is easy when we live by the principles of the word.

Life does not bring us trouble and sorrow directly. The years that life gives to us is what brings trouble and sorrow (Psalm 90:10). In like manner when life leaves, it takes with it trouble and sorrow. Only the Lord can bring us happiness and takes away sorrow. The blessings of the Lord are rich and adds no sorrow (Proverbs 10:22). The Lord allows life to give us time and take away time. Life is easy;

it comes and then goes without our effort or permission. The Lord gives, and the Lord takes away (Job 1:21). Living is hard because we have no control of life. It brings years and takes away years. No one can predict when it is coming or when it is leaving. Jesus controls life; it is up to us to live the way the Lord designed it to be. We owe this to God and ourselves.